I0225156

GRANDPARENTS
in the BIBLE

ELMER TOWNS

© Copyright 2023–Elmer L. Towns

All rights reserved. This book is protected by the copyright laws of the United States of America. This book may not be copied or reprinted for commercial gain or profit. The use of short quotations or occasional page copying for personal or group study is permitted and encouraged. Permission will be granted upon request. Unless otherwise identified, Scripture quotations are taken from the New King James Version. Copyright © 1982 by Thomas Nelson, Inc. Used by permission. All rights reserved. Scripture quotations marked NLT are taken from the Holy Bible, New Living Translation, copyright 1996, 2004, 2015. Used by permission of Tyndale House Publishers, Wheaton, Illinois 60189. All rights reserved.

All emphasis within Scripture quotations is the author's own. Please note that Destiny Image's publishing style capitalizes certain pronouns in Scripture that refer to the Father, Son, and Holy Spirit, and may differ from some publishers' styles.

DESTINY IMAGE® PUBLISHERS, INC.
P.O. Box 310, Shippensburg, PA 17257-0310
"Promoting Inspired Lives."

This book and all other Destiny Image and Destiny Image Fiction books are available at Christian bookstores and distributors worldwide.

For more information on foreign distributors, call 717-532-3040.

Reach us on the Internet: www.destinyimage.com.

ISBN 13 TP: 978-0-7684-7594-4

ISBN 13 eBook: 978-0-7684-7595-1

For Worldwide Distribution.

1 2 3 4 5 6 7 8 / 27 26 25 24 23

TABLE OF CONTENTS

PART THREE

Part Four

Part Five

INTRODUCTION

BEING a grandparent is one of the most fulfilling experiences in life, you fulfill the cycle God placed within each human. When a grandchild is born—either boy or girl—it means you have fulfilled God's plan of producing reproducers. "God created everything that is living but He didn't stop there. Just creating life was not His plan. God planned the future so that every living thing would reproduce itself. But that only guarantees two generations, i.e., first what God created and second what it reproduced. "Then God said, 'Let the earth produce every sort of animal, each producing offspring of the same kind.'" (Genesis 1:24, NLT). God created each with the ability to reproduce itself continually. "Seed-bearing plant, and trees that grow seed-bearing fruit. These seeds will then produce the kinds of plants and trees from which they came" (Genesis 1:11, NLT).

The same principles applied to Adam and Eve. "So, God created human beings...then God blessed them and said, 'Be fruitful and multiply. Fill the earth'" (Genesis 1:27-28, NLT). This is God's command for a husband and wife to have children and grandchildren and for the cycle to continue until the earth is filled with people.

Not everyone who has children gets to enjoy their grandchildren. Something could happen to a grandparent, so they don't live to see a grandchild. Or something could happen to the child, so they don't live to marry and have children. A child could die...or not marry or not have children...or other tragedies could happen. But being a grandparent is a fulfilling experience. The grandparent is a part of God's cycle, they are part of God's plan to reproduce...and fill the earth.

Grandparents get to show their grandchildren the world through their eyes, i.e., the world in which they lived...worked...ministered for God...and tried to improve for their generation. Grandparents first saw the world through their eyes, then second, they got to see the world through their grandchildren's eyes. They first lived in their world then again, they lived in the second-generation culture and helped their children live in the culture of their generation.

But grandchildren stretch the grandparents to live in the third-generation culture of their grandchildren. Now grandparents have to do it again with their grandchildren. They must help their children raise their children in a culture that may be different from what both of them experienced.

Hopefully, grandparents can live to see again God's miracle of birth, growth, and achievement. What they did poorly or wrong with their children, perhaps they can help guide properly the grandchildren, so they turn out better...smarter...more advanced...and more spiritual.

Grandparents have experienced more than the two preceding generations. They should be able to give wiser counsel to the children, so the grandchildren are also smarter...more advanced...and more spiritual.

Grandparents—you have produced reproducers. You can pass your heritage on to your grandchildren. Why? So, they can do more for God...and do it better...and do it longer...because your grandchildren are carrying on your legacy.

In this book you will learn how Jacob, the youthful rebel, was confronted by God. He made long-range investments for the future for God's people. We see at the end Jacob's life he understood responsibility and passed the family heritage on to his grandchildren.

We see Naomi with her husband turning their backs on God's land. That left the Holy Land and God's influence to go live in a land of idols. They sought money, prestige, and easy living. She let her sons marry heathen women. Then disaster came. Her husband died, later her sons died, leaving her with two daughters-in-law. In her senior years Naomi came back to her heritage and returned to her roots. God gave Naomi a second chance through her grandson Obed. She dedicated her grandmother years to raise her grandson for God. He became the grandfather to King David.

Asa's father and grandfather were compromising kings of Judah that influenced God's people to worship idols. Asa's grandmother Maachah was even worse. The grandson Asa led God's people in revival and reestablished temple worship. This chapter is a warning against grandparents who exercised evil influence on their grandchildren. But it is also a promise that God can raise up a godly leader—in spite of an ungodly heritage—to lead his people in returning to God in a revival.

Noah was a man of faith in God who built a boat to save the world. After the flood, Noah became a farmer and sinned at the end of his life. His grandson also sinned. Both positive and negative influence of Grandfather Noah is seen in this chapter.

Lois was the godly grandmother who raised her daughter Eunice to live the same way. Both ladies were married to unsaved Gentiles. They were living on the edge of Roman civilization in the mountains of modern-day Turkey. Apparently, there was not enough Jews in Lystra to organize a synagogue. With very little help and support the grandmother and mother trained Timothy so that he became a godly leader in the early church.

The final grandparent in this book is Paul. His role is seen in Second Timothy 2:2. This verse is called the principle of "producing reproducers." Paul produced Timothy who produced a third generation of "faithful men" who produced a fourth generation of Christians called "others."

PART ONE

GRANDPARENTS IN THE BIBLE

HOW TO BE A
"GREAT" GRANDPARENT

THIS section is not about the fourth generation, i.e., great-grandparents. No! That is a wonderful topic, and if grandparents would be all God wants of them, they will see their fourth generation serving Jesus Christ.

This section is about the first generation, it is about you becoming a "great" grandparent. It is about becoming better than you expect, or even better than you have talents to become. The word "great" in great grandparent is to make it stand apart like you a grandparent can stand apart. The word great means to become greater than your talents, and greater than expected.

It's Christ who makes you "great," so this section focuses on seven principles to make any grandparent a "great" grandparent.

The second lesson on Jacob focuses on the task of blessing his grandchildren. Next Naomi, grandmother to Obed was given a second chance by the God of the second chances. Asa became a revival king in spite of an evil grandmother. Then Noah who blessed his two sons, Shem and Japheth, but not his son Ham, while cursing a grandson Canaan. Grandmother Lois had faith that she poured into her daughter Eunice, and together the two women influenced Timothy to become an early church missionary with the apostle Paul. Finally, Paul is persecuted as a grandparent teaching Timothy who taught the spiritual grandchildren faith _____. They in turn extended it to future generations, i.e., others.

1. Become a Radical Disciple
2. Dedicate Yourself to be a Devoted Disciple
3. A Disciple-Maker by Example
4. A Disciple-Maker by Become Necessary
5. A Disciple-Maker by Pouring Yourself into Them
6. A Disciple-Maker by Intentional Instructions

Chapter One

THROUGH THE EYES OF GRANDCHILDREN

Y OU know grandchildren say the funniest things about their grandparents. As an illustration, a youngster said, "everyone should have a grandmother because they let you watch television and they watch with you. They are not like your parents who don't have time to spend watching what you want to see, they only watch what they want to see."

Another grandchild said, "Grandparents are funny because they take their teeth out." Another one said that grandparents are really smart. They can answer questions like who is God, and where is God, and how come God is not married?

Still others said I like grandparents the most, because when they read to us, they don't skip words. They don't mind if we ask them to read the same story over...and over...and over again.

SOURCE OF THE TERM "GRAND"

When a youngster was asked where his grandfather worked, he said, "My grandfather doesn't have to do anything, but he is there when I go to see him. Then he and grandma take me to the store, buy me ice cream and they drive really slow."

Did you know that grandparents have interesting names? Grandpa for instance can be called grandpa, grandpapa, grandad, granddaddy, pops, poppy, or pawpaw.

What about grandmother, she is sometimes called, grandmama, grandma, granny, nannie, nana, memaw, and grammy.

When children have two sets of living grandparents, i.e., both maternal and fraternal, they usually call their grandparents and add a first name such as Grandpa George, Grandma Joan. Usually they don't add the family as Grandma Smith, Grandpa Jones.

When you look at history, where did the term *grandparents* come from? Let's begin with the word *grand*. Technically it comes from an old use of the term in French; *graunde* or Latin; *magnus,* which could mean *older* or *elder*. Therefore, when you talk about your father, you use the word father. But when you speak about an earlier generation you are speaking about an old father or a grandfather.

ROLE OF GRANDPARENTS

The role of grandparents is changing in our contemporary world and they are becoming increasingly involved in raising their grandchildren. In the last 10 years, around one-third of the children in the United States live in a household consisting of both parents and at least one grandparent. However, according to statistics in Europe around 40% of grandparents take care of their grandchildren in the absence of the parent(s). However, jump across the English Channel to Britain and you will find about 63% of grandparents care for their grandchildren who are under 16 years of age.

Recently, we have seen in the United States grandparents becoming more involved with their grandchildren. Why is that? First, life expectancy has increased while fertility rates have decreased. That means there are more children growing up while their grandparents are still living. Therefore, their grandparents can have an influence in their lives.

But also decrease in fertility rates means grandparents can devote more attention and resources to fewer children or just one child.

One more thing about the contemporary role of grandparents. With more mothers involved in the workforce, caregiving of the children falls to the grandparents.

But also, the growing numbers of single parent families increases the need of support by grandparents for childcare.

DIFFERENT TYPES OF GRANDPARENT INVOLVEMENT

There are different types of grandparent involvement with their grandchildren. This includes nonresident grandparents, then Coresident grandparentsliving in the home with a parent(s) and grandchildren, and then grandparent-maintained households where they take care of the children. Finally, there are custodial grandparents where the grandchildren are given to the grandparents to raise.

Nonresident grandparents. This involves grandparents who do not live with their grandchildren, but they provide care in their house such as picking them up from school, feeding them the evening meal, and doing babysitting and/or other chores until the parent(s) come to pick up the children.

Coresident grandparents. This is either the grandfather or grandmother living with their grandchildren and their parents. This household is known as a three-generational household. According to the 2010 census, this type of household is more likely to identify with those in lower class income, poverty, or those grandparents who suffer from a disability or illness.

Grandparent-maintained household. In this illustration the grandparent(s) are in charge of the household and take care of running the household. One or two of the parents may live with them, and as a result the grandparents are looking after the grandchildren who happens to be in that household. Again, the 2010 census indicates that 33% of the American children live in a grandparent-maintained household, this is comparable to 30% who either live with a grandmother or grandfather and one or more parents.

Custodial grandparents. These are grandparent(s) who raise their grandchildren without the presence of either parent(s). You may find this more common among ethnic groups or minority groups. Again, going back to the 2010 census, around 50% of the custodial grandparents in the U.S. belong to an ethnic or minority group. This is probably because the grandparents have been given legal custody care of the children or will assume that role because the grandchildren are neglected or abused, or their parents are unable to provide for them. This may be caused by alcohol and drug addiction, or the parents have died, or are incarcerated, or in some cases parents are not able financially to take care of the children, but in some cases, they remain in contact with them.

Grandparents have different functions with their grandchildren in different societies and cultures. First, they provided instrumental care for them such as picking them up from school and feeding them, taking them to appointments such as school, doctor, sports, etc. These grandparents supply emotional support and give stability for the child growing up. In these situations, the grandparents protect the children from being negatively impacted by culture such as harsh parenting, poor finances, single parent families that have come from fracture. What do grandparents do in these roles, they communicate values, help with schoolwork, giving direction and council, dealing with personal problems of the children, etc.

Research shows that children who have a close relationship with their grandparents and/or raised by grandparents, tend to have better well-being, personalities, and experience fewer emotional problems, demonstrate fewer juvenile behavior problems; they also tend to be more academically engaged, or more likely to help others, and have a good attitude toward adults in general. One of the negative factors is that studies show that children who are under the care of their grandparents tend to have certain poor health issues such as obesity and other problems from being overweight.

Taking care of grandchildren is a high demanding job that requires constant attention, constant energy, and the devotion of time. Therefore, grandparents who are involved in raising their grandchildren could have a negative impact on the health of grandparents, both physical and emotional. That means they have a higher chance of suffering from physical health issues because they focus their health attention to their grandchildren.

Also, there are emotional issues involved when raising grandchildren. Because there are physical issues as well as highly emotional issues, involved in raising young children, this could produce a stressful and overwhelming experience for grandparents. Resulting in a negative impact on the grandparent such as anxiety, depression, or other causes of mental distress.

Another issue is that grandparents taking care of their grandchildren are forced to limit their social relationships with other older adults their age. In doing so, grandparents become isolated from activities with older adults.

Fear of death is another issue usually addressed when speaking to grandparents, because they realize they are the primary guide and influence for their grandchildren. They become stressed over their grandchildren's future well-being because they think they may become disabled or they will not be present to help their grandchildren. Their thinking will cause emotional problems in the grandparents. In turn that brings more stress and physical health problems into the grandparent's life.

However, quickly let's note there are many positive advantages of taking care of grandchildren. Because grandparents are giving long hours of caregiving to their grandchildren, they are also keeping alive their cognitive functions. To be specific, taking care of grandchildren keeps them sharper in mental awareness, relationship to the community, the outside world, and relationship to cultural changes. They understand adaption to cultural changes that are being made now and that their grandchildren must adapt to change. But also, grandparents who are frequently interacting with grandchildren reduce the cognitive aging process associated with dementia. What does that mean? grandparents who welcome grandchildren by caring for them or spending time with them will live longer and healthier.

Another issue is that grandparents looking after their grandchildren will have stronger emotional health. As an example, they will have a feeling of purpose in life again after retirement because they are needed, and they are doing something they want to do. Remember, they have raised their children and now they have a new purpose in life to raise their grandchildren. That new challenge also gives them another chance to correct any mistakes they may have made raising their children. As an illustration, many grandparents make sure to give the love to their grandchildren that they did not show to their own children. Why is this? Because the parents are the primary disciplinarian. Therefore, parents must deal with negative responses of children, as well as all of the positive responses. However, in the grandparenting experience, their response is mostly positive.

Another issue is that grandparents can take care of certain needs of grandchildren. Of course, when there are financial needs, they step in to help. But there are other times when a grandchild may become involved in sexual abuse, incarceration, emotional problems, and/or parental death. It is then the grandparents can help with that need.

At this time look at the ethnic differences in families. You will find many ethnic groups are more likely to provide guidance and discipline to their grandchildren due to their cultural family structure. In these ethnic groups, usually relatives, nonblood kin as well as distant relatives may live together in the family. This is true especially among African American families as well as Latino families living in the U.S.

They have a strong preference to live together as a family group. They want to keep strong family contact because most of them were brought up that away having come a second, or third-generation family as they immigrated to the U.S.

It has been noted that Caucasian grandparents are less likely to have as great an influence on their grandchildren than an ethnic household. That is because Caucasians tend to establish different households. However, we find ethnic families have a higher care giving roll to grandparents because they tend to live together and expect to live together. Living with grandparents is part of their culture.

Psychologists have noted that Caucasian grandparents tend to deal with their grandchildren in a cognitive or directive way when it comes to social contact, talking, and counseling. However, often African American and Latino grandparents rely more on tradition, instruction, and at times punishment when grandchildren do not meet cultural standards.

TRUE PURPOSE OF GRANDPARENTING VERSES MYTHS

The first myth is that grandparents are there primarily to enjoy their grandchildren, to see them once or twice a week, give them cookies, bring them presents, and provide money.

The second myth is that grandparenting is a leisure time of life. You don't have to worry about disciplining your children, and certainly not grandchildren. This myth tells you that the role of grandparents is to retire...relax...enjoy life...because that is what they promised themselves.

However, the primary role of grandparents is to communicate family heritage that they have received from the parents and grandparents. Heritage communication is the primary role of grandparenting.

Having said the chief role of grandparents is communicating family heritage, most grandparents are clueless how they can influence their grandchildren for God, almost the same way they were clueless how they could use godly influence for their own children. What they did for their own children will reproduce in their own grandchildren if they are not helped. The benefit of this book, *Grandparents in the Bible* tells you how grandparents can be positive influencers on their grandchildren and their children.

SIX PLACES TO BEGIN

1. *Bless the grandchildren*. More than anything else the grandparents can bless their grandchildren with the expectation of God in their lives and the challenge of God's plan for their lives. Blessing spiritually is more than giving money, things, or food. By the time you are in your 40s or above, grandparents should bear spiritual security in their faith in God and walk with Him. They should have a ministry for God and their grandchildren should know it. Grandparents are over all the emotional tensions of their teenage years as well as the emotional tensions of adjusting to one another in marriage and a new baby in their family. Therefore, grandparents can have a stable influence on the life of their grandchildren. In chapter two Jacob blesses his grandchildren when he lays his hands on their head to

bless them. Jacob is communicating heritage. By that we mean he is communicating his expectations of what God is going to do in the future. But Jacob also communicates who they are in the present, and what future God has for them. Therefore, when grandparents bless their grandchildren, they tie the past to the future. Hence, the greatest role of grandparents is communicating family heritage.

2. *Leave a legacy*. One of the greatest contributions of grandparents is leaving their legacy to their children. Walk into a home of grandparents and you see souvenirs everywhere. Also, pictures; lots of pictures! Usually pictures of weddings, events, birthdays, etc.; history is posted all over the house. Grandparents should take time to explain to their grandchildren what happened in these pictures...why it happened...and the good things that happened because of the event. Then grandparents should talk to them about other events in the house. Maybe souvenirs of trips. Communicate to grandchildren where they went...what they learned...and what they experienced. In that they build expectations that their grandchildren will go to those places...learn the same thing... and have the same experience.

3. *Grandparents should talk about their heritage*. Talk about their first home when they got married, and their first child and what they learned from having children. As they walk around telling grandchildren about furniture in the house and kitchen utensils as well as chairs and other things in the house, explaining the meaning behind all them. Were they gifts at Christmas time, or birthday presents? Explain to the children what happened in these events, so you immerse grandchildren in the past. Because when they have a past, it is a base for their future.

4. *Leave your grandchildren a legacy*. When they get the phone call saying grandpa died, what will they remember most about grandpa? It should be more than the money he gave them, or the ice cream he bought them. They should remember

what grandpa accomplished in his life, where he learned many lessons, how he served in the church, and the job he did for his vocation. They should know and remember their grandparents. Why? Because most will go to a funeral for their grandparents.

5. *Carrying the torch*. What is a torch? It is your life. A torch is what you were and what you accomplished. The gospel is a torch. A torch is something grandparents received, and believed, and that torch changed their life. Jesus Christ transformed them, therefore; make sure Jesus transforms your grandchildren. So, when you pass the torch on, you are not passing on a catechism or a building where you attended Sunday school. No! You are passing on your belief in Jesus Christ. You pass on what you lived for and what you died for. So, pass on the torch. Don't drop it...hide it...don't change it. The torch is Jesus Christ and He is the light of the world. The torch is that burning light that guided your life and you want your grandchildren to live by the light of that same torch! You want your grandchildren to live for God just as you did. Also, you want your grandchildren to love the church and serve in the church, attend church and give financially to the church. Therefore, grandparents need to tell their grandchildren about the ministry they have done in the church. Stories of their getting saved...getting awards in Sunday school...joining the church...Baptism...first communion. But most of all grandparents need to tell their grandchildren how they led their children to Christ. This is the grandchildren's mother and father. Tell the story of the conversion of their parents as well as the conversion of the grandparents. Those stories should ultimately lead to the conversion of the next generation of children born to your grandchildren.

6. *Communicate a standard of moral living in an immoral world*. Grandparents must be a GPS to their grandchildren. That means a spiritual guiding principle for the whole family. Just

as grandparents had to face issues growing up whether they would drink alcohol or remain pure sexually till they got married—the issues they faced—their grandchildren will face. Therefore, you communicate why you lived for God. If the Ten Commandments are important to you; communicate that to the grandchildren. Learn to ask questions and listen for *teachable moments*.

TEN POINTS OF LIGHT FOR GRANDPARENTS

1. *Grandparents can best show a vision of the future*. The key to influencing a grandchild's future...is the past. Both your past and their parents' past. What God has done in the past; God can do for your grandchildren as they grow older. Help them look at the future through the lenses of the past and learn from the past. Then make sure they put on the glasses of failure. Talk about the thing you did wrong and the things you would do differently. Talk about your failures, so your grandchildren will not make the same mistakes. But now it is important to talk about successes. Think of the few things in life that you have done well. Think of the attendance pins you won at church, tell the grandchildren about those. Also, think of awards you won in Scouts, Awana, high school, sports, or wherever. Tell them about those victories that influenced your life. Not bragging but tell them what you have done that they can do. Also, tell stories of great vacations, great church events, or great revivals. Tell them about your first apartment or building your first home. Let the grandchildren enter your achievements so they can dream with you and maybe they will find their dreams.

2. *Grandparents are effective because they get a second chance*. Sometimes raising children is difficult and we all make mistakes. Therefore, the grandparents can realize what they did wrong

and they can do it differently with grandchildren. They should be careful that they don't tell all the weaknesses of their parents. You don't want to put their parents down at the eyes of their children. But point out the lessons they learned through their failures and success. In the same way your grandchildren will learn through their failures and success. Grandparenting is a second chance. That means the things you did wrong with your children; God has given you a second chance to do it differently with your grandchildren. You can be more loving...more forgiving...more availabile...and more compassionate. There is an old song grandparents sang when they were teens that says, "Love is sweeter...the second time around...love is sweeter with both feet on the ground." Therefore, your love for your grandchildren will be sweeter than perhaps then for your children. Remember you don't have to deal with all the negatives that parents have to deal with. You're a grandparent, you can look at all the positive of your grandchildren. What happens when you become a grandparent, you have more common sense, you know how to do things practically, you have both feet on the ground.

3. _Grandparents set a moral example for grandchildren._ One of my favorite heroes at the Saturday matinee with the double feature are cartoons was the cowboy shows. John Wayne was my all-time favorite. The advice I heard him give on film, I will pass on to you. "Life is tough, but it is tougher when you are stupid." I never forgot it is tough being stupid. If you are not stupid... and you don't do stupid things...and don't say stupid things, and you don't respond in a stupid way, life is much easier. So, what do we learn? It is much easier to live for God, than to sin. It is much easier to do right, but it's stupid to do wrong.

4. _Grandparents are more like God than when they were parents._ As parents they had to set the standards for family and community living. That meant everyone who lived in their house had to live by their rules, therefore being a parent is being a rule maker, rule keeper, and you have to deal with rule breaking. But that also leads to being a rule punisher for those who break the rules. Of course, parents reward good behavior and love their children. But they are forced into a dual role of both punishing that which is wrong and rewarding that which is right. But grandparents are not in that dual role, they listen to grandchildren...they give good things to their grandchildren...they play with their grandchildren...they are patient...they show grace...they overlook faults...and they don't yell at or punish their grandchildren. Remember, grandparents are like God, He does not mock, He doesn't put you down, He doesn't criticize you. God just speaks and expects you to understand.

5. _The joy of grandparenting is blessing them._ When you bless them what do you do? You add value to their life.

6. _Grandparents communicate values and attitudes of tradition._ What are they doing when communicating family values and attitudes? They are passing heritage into the lives of their grandchildren. When we talk about values, we are not always talking about right or wrong, i.e., sin. We are talking about the way the family does things, i.e., the kind of car they drive, the kind of dessert they serve, the kind of vacation they enjoy, and the way they spend their money, and the television shows the family watches together. These things make up the values of life. So, grandparents communicate these values and attitudes best by the gifts they give, but not just the gifts, but explaining why they were given and how grandchildren can use them. When two of my grandchildren were small, I bought each of them a share of stock around $5,000 each. I purchased them stock from the Dow Jones Stock Market. I wanted them to use the profit from the stock market to go to college. I probably made one mistake, I bought different shares of stock

for the grandson, than for the granddaughter. When they graduated from high school, I gave it to them. The problem was the $5,000 I spent on the granddaughter went down in value and was worth $2,400. She was disappointed and cashed it in immediately and paid off her credit card bill. The grandson's stock from different companies increased from $5,000 to over $26,000. He hasn't touched it, saving it for when he really needs it.

7. *How they feel about their grandchildren is how grandchildren will feel about themselves*. The way we criticize or punish a child or grandchild, will determine their self-perception, and that will determine their actions. If you tell a child you are dumb, or you are always dirty; when a child brings home a bad report card and you say, you always make bad grades, you are tearing down that child. When you tell a child he is dumb, he will go through life thinking I am dumb. That child may not try to make the honor roll or try to make the best grades in class because he thinks, "I am dumb." Look at it through spiritual eyes. When you tell a child, they are a terrible sinner, or they have a dirty mouth, you are creating a negative self-image. When you always make a child feel they wear a dunce cap and they are sitting in the corner being punished, what does that say about their view of spirituality? They think they are unspiritual, unloved, and unnecessary for God. But at the same time when you commend a child a positive self-perception, you influence what they think of themselves and how they behave. The mother who always says to her daughter, "you are so pretty" or "I love how you dress," or she tells her little girl how pretty she is all the time, the girl will dress "pretty" according to self-perception. If you tell a boy he is smart, he will try to find a way to study hard to make you proud of him. When you raise the child's self-esteem, they will perceive themselves that way and act that way. Parents and grandparents can radically form the way children think about

themselves. When you always fuss at a child for breaking the rules, for always coming home late, for always sneaking behind your back, what is that child going to do? They are going to act according to the way they see themselves. They will sneak behind your back and do what you don't want them to do.

8. *God has a plan for each grandchild, and it is the responsibility of the grandparents to help them find that plan*. You must begin teaching every child and grandchild that God has a plan for that child. God has said, "For I know the thoughts that I think toward you, says the Lord, thoughts of peace and not of evil, to give you a future and a hope." (Jeremiah 29:11, NKJV). When a child/grandchild realizes God has a plan just for them, it tends to make them special in God's sight, and raise their desire to please the Lord. When I was around eight or nine years old picking cotton in my grandpa's farm in Sardinia, South Carolina, Bobby Johnson said something to me that I never forgot. Grandpa owned the field and supplied the tools, seed, and fertilizer; and the sharecroppers did all the work. In the end they split the profits. I was picking cotton for a penny a pound. In one day, I could pick around 60 pounds of cotton, so I received 60 cents for working in the hot sun from eight in the morning until about two in the afternoon. One day we were resting at the end of a row and Johnson said to me. "Captain, you are going to make a preacher someday." The other sharecroppers cautioned, "Be careful Bobby, that is the grandson, you will get in trouble." "No"...Bobby continued, "Captain you have a tender heart toward God and the things of heaven. I can tell you are going to be a preacher. One day when you get to be a preacher, I want you to come and preach in my church and I will introduce you to my congregation." I never forgot what Bobby Johnson told me I could be a preacher. I thought about it during junior and senior high school. I was not yet a Christian, and cussed all the time,

but knew it was wrong. In God's time I was saved after I graduated from high school on July 25, 1950. I knew when I was saved that God had called me into fulltime service.

9. *Grandparents can be the most patient generation even though a few are grouchy*. Most children get along well with their grandparents because the older generation is kind and gentle and not condemning. A bond is usually established between the grandparents and the grandchild. Therefore, grandparents should use that leverage to teach the child about family heritage and how they—the grandchildren—fit into that heritage. Remember, family heritage grows when children know their roots and where their family came from. They need to know those who influenced them. Then, family heritage grows when children are pointed to the future, and the influence they can make on their children. Make sure grandparents tell their grandchildren what they can do for God and His Kingdom.

10. *Grandparents can be a bridge over troubled water*. Because grandparents are kind and loving, when grandchildren get in trouble, they can go talk with a grandparent. Sometimes it is not talking about their troubles, they just want to talk about life, the future, or whatever is on their mind. These conversations can have eternal results. God can use the gentleness of grandparenting to capture the heart of the young, then point them in the way of godliness. Since grandparents can be a *Bridge Over Troubled Water*, the words of the popular song by Simon and Garfunkel can have a lasting meaning upon the grandchild.

Chapter Two

JACOB: GRANDFATHER OF EPHRAIM AND MANASSEH

A Grandfather Blesses His Grandchildren

Grandfather – Jacob

Father – Joseph

Grandsons – Manasseh and Ephraim

"Then Israel stretched out his right hand and laid it on Ephraim's head, who was the younger, and his left hand on Manasseh's head, guiding his hands knowingly, for Manasseh was the firstborn...The Angel who has redeemed me from all evil, Bless the lads; Let my name be named upon them, the name of my fathers Abraham and Isaac; And let them grow into a multitude in the midst of the earth. Now when Joseph saw that his father laid his right hand on the head of Ephraim, it displeased him; so he took hold of his father's hand to remove it from Ephraim's head to Manasseh's head. And Joseph said to his father, 'Not so, my father, for this one is the firstborn; put your right hand on his head.' But his father refused and said, 'I know, my son, I know. He also shall become a people, and he also shall be great; but truly his younger brother shall be greater than he, and his descendants shall become a multitude of nations'" (Genesis 48:14, 16-19).

THE footsteps echoed off the white marbled walls of the palace; young Ephraim was running through the halls to his brother's bedroom. Ephraim was the youngest son of Joseph, who was the minister of agriculture in Egypt, second to Pharaoh. His black flashing eyes reflected his father Joseph, a Hebrew; his fair skin reflected his mother, an Egyptian. Because of his father's wealth, servants were stationed everywhere throughout his palace and both boys had a private attendant.

"Manasseh," the younger boy yelled out the name of his older and larger brother, "Guess where we're going today?" His exciting yell turned the servants' heads. Ephraim burst into his brother's bedroom to announce,

"We're going to see Grandpa Jacob today."

Ephraim was barely winded. He was the more athletic of the two boys, also the more daring, the more aggressive and when it came to curiosity, Ephraim was the one who always got into trouble. Joseph felt that Ephraim was more like his Grandfather Jacob than any of his 12 sons.

Ephraim and Manasseh huddled with excitement to leave the boring city and travel to Grandpa Jacob's farm country in the Nile delta where everything was green, lush and there were sheep and cows everywhere. In the city where the boys lived, white stone buildings rose from the white surrounding sand. Everything was dry...hot...arid.

Grandpa Jacob always told stories of traveling to the far nation of Mesopotamia and being a shepherd and sleeping on the ground, under the stars. His tales of killing wild predators thrilled the boys, as well as his stories about fighting and taking the city Shechem and Mount Gerizim. The boys' other grandfather, Potipherah, priest of On, worshiped the Egyptian god Re. When their mother Asenaph took them to visit her father, Grandpa Potipherah, he tried to teach them the Egyptian names of the different stars and how to worship the stars.

But the boys believed in Grandpa Jacob's God, not Grandpa Potipherah's god.

As the chariot rumbled through the burning sands of the Egyptian Desert, they saw camels—the desert travelers. As they got closer to Grandpa Jacob's home, the landscape slowly changed to the green pastures of the Nile delta where they saw sheep and cattle grazing in green fields.

A rank of soldiers headed the procession; they went everywhere with Joseph, not so much for protection, but as a statement of prestige. Behind the boys came servants and other Egyptian dignitaries.

Grandpa Jacob knew the boys were coming, so he had forced himself to get dressed, slipping into his comfortable shepherd's tunic faded with age, rumpled, and worn. Like most old people, Jacob didn't pay attention to his clothes for he didn't see well, and style didn't matter when you're ready to die. The coat had the smell of sheep and perspiration, but old people don't smell as well as when they were younger; Jacob wore clothes that were comfortable.

Joseph greeted his father warmly, as he had always done. Egyptian scribes were along to record the events, for the last words of great men were important for posterity.

Joseph had brought the best doctors available in the palace. They knew the latest cures and could mix many herbs and potions. But old Jacob shook his head "No" to the doctor; he relied on the techniques he had learned in the field, shepherding his sheep.

Jacob took control of the meeting, telling everyone, "When I was a young man running away from home, God Almighty appeared to me in a mountain named Bethel—it means the "House of God"—and I needed reassurance from the LORD. My brother Esau wanted to kill me. That night God appeared to me in a dream saying,

"'*Behold, I the Lord will prosper you in all that you do, I will give you many children, and you will become a great nation. I the Lord promise this land to you—a promised land—that you shall inherit this land for an everlasting possession.'"*

Then Jacob told the part of the story that hurt. He told how his sons hated Joseph and tried to kill Joseph but sold him into slavery. In slavery, God protected Joseph and elevated him to rule over all the agriculture of Egypt.

Then Grandfather Jacob abruptly asked, "Are these your two sons—Ephraim and Manasseh—who were born to you in the land of Egypt before I came here?"

Then Jacob made the pronouncement that the two grandsons would be adopted by him. Even though Ephraim and Manasseh were half Egyptian, old Jacob wanted everyone to know that these two boys would have a Hebrew inheritance, so he announced before all, "These boys are mine." Then he turned to the scribes noting,

"Write it down, just as I said."

To make sure that they all understood, Jacob continued, "These two boys are mine, just as much as Reuben and Simeon are mine."

Again, Jacob turned to the scribes noting, "These shall be placed in order after their brethren in my inheritance."

Even though Joseph was one of the richest men in Egypt, and Joseph could give his sons more wealth than Jacob ever conceived, it was important for the old man to give the boys something. Jacob's inheritance was important because every one of his sheep and cattle were given by God. When a few things are all that the man has, these few things are important to him and to his grandsons. And in giving to his grandsons what he had, Jacob was giving them his identity, his character, and his life.

"Bring your sons to me," Jacob said, pointing to Ephraim and Manasseh. The situation that followed was filled with tension, for Joseph knew what should be done, but wily old Jacob knew what he would do.

Joseph brought the boys to his father, according to their birth order. Jacob's left hand was to be on the head of younger Ephraim, his second born. Jacob's right hand—the hand of authority—was to be on the head of Manasseh, his first born. Then Joseph bowed his head. As the boys approached, Jacob crossed his arms, placing his right hand on the head of Ephraim who was the younger and his left hand to Manasseh, the older. The old grandfather blessed his grandsons;

"Lord, You redeemed me from the evil one, now Lord, protect these young boys from evil. Let my name be on them, and let my inheritance, be their inheritance. May the name of Abraham, Isaac, and Jacob be upon these boys and may they grow into a multitude on the earth."

When Joseph looked up, he saw that Jacob's right hand was on Ephraim, the younger son. He objected saying, "Not so, father, you have your hand of blessing on Ephraim, but he is the second born."

Jacob didn't respond, but smiled inwardly, knowing he was doing God's will. He told Joseph, "Remember God's principle of choice. When I was born second, the Lord told my mother that the *older shall serve the younger,* meaning the second born will rule the first born." That day Jacob gave Ephraim the spiritual birthright, which included the spiritual leadership of the family clan, as well as the right to pray for all the family.

Jacob could not have known what would happen to Ephraim, but God knew. One day the entire nation of Israel would be called by the name *Ephraim,* and one day the tribe of Ephraim would have more people than any other tribe, and more soldiers than any of the other twelve tribes of Israel. The prosperity of the tribe of Ephraim would flow into all of the other eleven tribes, making each of them wealthy and rich.

But not to leave Manasseh out, Jacob explained to Joseph, "Manasseh will be a great people, he will become a great nation, but his young brother Ephraim will be a greater people and the children of Ephraim shall lead the children of Manasseh."

"Write what I have said," Jacob again turned to the scribes and said, and they did.

"Behold, I die!" Grandpa Jacob told everyone in the room.

When Jacob used the word *death,* no one knew whether he meant minutes...hours...days...or even years. But somehow in their hearts, they knew death was imminent. Jacob added a final blessing for all his family,

"God will be with you, and bring the nation out of Egypt back into the Promised Land; because God promised, He will take you back to the land of our fathers."

WHAT CAN A GRANDFATHER DO?

Lessons to Take Away

When grandparents can't spend most time with their grandchildren, or give them much material inheritance, their greatest gift can be to spiritually bless and pray for their grandchildren.

What could Grandpa Jacob give his grandchildren? He was poor in worldly goods compared to their wealthy father Joseph. They lived in a palace, had access to the best Universities of Egypt, had household servants, and all of the symbols of power. Grandfather Jacob had nothing to give his grandchildren but *the blessing* that God gave him.

Jacob was an absentee grandfather that his grandchildren seldom saw. The children of Joseph lived in the city where Joseph was minister of agriculture for Egypt. Grandpa Jacob lived far removed in the Nile delta, in rural conditions; a completely different way of life. When a grandfather doesn't see his son very often, he can give them a *spiritual inheritance* because God is everywhere, and he can transcend boundaries to touch the lives of his grandchildren.

What could physically weak Jacob do for his grandchildren? When a grandfather can no longer walk down a trail with his grandchildren, nor is he physically able to sit and talk with his grandchildren. When they come for a visit, what can he do? A grandfather can put *his name* upon them, as well as the *name of the Lord*; Who will always be with the grandchildren.

What can a grandfather give to his grandchildren when he has nothing left to give? The most important thing that you give to your grandchildren is not money, possessions, or even the homestead. The most important thing is a *spiritual heritage* to guide their life.

FOUR THINGS GRANDPA JACOB SAID TO THEM

1. *Grandpa Jacob gave his testimony to his grandsons.* When the boys finally arrived at Jacob's home, and he was ready for an important audience with them, Jacob gave the boys his testimony. Had the boys heard the testimony before? Did they know it by heart? That's not the issue. Jacob thought it was important to *rehearse* for them what God has done for him. Grandpa Jacob began, "God Almighty appeared to me at Luz in the land of Canaan and blessed me" (Gen. 48:3). Was Grandpa Jacob sharing his salvation experience? Was Grandpa Jacob just telling his grandsons about a life-changing experience? Jacob told the boys how he met God at Bethel.

WHAT HAPPENED WHEN GOD MET JACOB AT BETHEL

"Now Jacob went out from Beersheba and went toward Haran. So he came to a certain place and stayed there all night, because the sun had set. And he took one of the stones of that place and put it at his head, and he lay down in that place to sleep. Then he dreamed, and behold, a ladder was set up on the earth, and its top reached to heaven; and there the angels of God were ascending and descending on it. And behold, the LORD stood above it and said: "I am the LORD God of Abraham your father and the God of Isaac; the land on which you lie I will give to you and your descendants. Also your descendants shall be as the dust of the earth; you shall spread abroad to the west and the east, to the north and the south; and in you and in your seed all the families of the earth shall be blessed. Behold, I am with you and will keep you wherever you go, and will bring you back to this land; for I will not leave you until I have done what I have spoken to you." Then Jacob awoke from his sleep and said, "Surely the LORD is in this place, and I did not know it." And he was afraid and said, "How awesome is this place! This is none other than the house of God, and this is the gate of heaven!" Then Jacob rose early in the morning, and took the stone that he had put at his head, set it up as a pillar, and poured oil on top of it. And he called the name of that place Bethel; but the name of that city had been Luz previously. Then Jacob made a vow, saying, "If God will be with me, and keep me in this way that I am going, and give me bread to eat and clothing to put on, so that I come back to my father's house in peace, then the LORD shall be my God. And this stone which I have set as a pillar shall be God's house, and of all that You give me I will surely give a tenth to You" (Genesis 28:10-22).

Grandfathers like to tell stories over and over, just as much as grandchildren like to hear them repeatedly. When Manasseh and Ephraim visited their grandfather—perhaps for the last time—Jacob thought that it was important to tell the boys about his encounter with God. "God, before whom my fathers Abraham and Isaac walked, the God who has fed me all my life long to this day" (Gen. 48:15).

WHAT'S INVOLVED IN GIVING YOUR TESTIMONY?

1. What you were before salvation.
2. What you did to receive Christ.
3. How you were changed.

2. *Jacob told the boys about God.* Jacob reminded them that God's name was "God Almighty" (v. 3). Today there is power in the name of Jesus, as well as healing in Jesus' name, deliverance in Jesus' name, and answered prayer in Jesus' name (Acts 3:6; 4:12; 5:28; John 14:13, 14). Tell your grandchildren what the name of Jesus means to you.

Today grandparents can tell their grandchildren stories from the Bible, but Jacob didn't have a Bible. He had to quote from memory what God said.

Jacob shared with his grandsons what God expected him to do. You must tell your grandchildren that God expects them to believe in Him, live for Him, and to grow as a Christian. In a real sense, today you must challenge your grandchildren to believe in Christ for salvation, live by the Word of God, and prepare themselves for Heaven.

3. *Grandpa Jacob told them the four-fold promise of God.* Jacob reminded the young boys of God's

promise to him. Much of the original promises of God to Abraham were repeated to Jacob. Jacob was the one through whom the blessing of God would come.

"Behold, I the Lord will prosper you in all that you do, I will give you many children, and you will become a great nation. I the Lord promise this land to you—a promise land—that you shall inherit this land for an everlasting possession" (adapted from Gen. 48:4).

4. *Grandpa Jacob told them about their grandmother.* Since grandmother Rachel was not present when Jacob passed the birthright on to the next generation, Grandpa Jacob had to remind his grandsons about her. He said, "When I came from Padan, Rachel died beside me in the land of Canaan on the way, when there was but a little distance to go to Ephrath; and I buried her there" (Gen. 48:7).

It's important that both grandfather and grandmother include the other when blessing their grandchildren. The love and care that grandparents have for each other, should extend to grandchildren. And not just love, their combined wisdom, prayers, financial, and spiritual inheritance.

WHAT JACOB SAID ABOUT THEIR GRANDMOTHER

1. Your grandmother died in travel.
2. I was there when she died.
3. We were almost home.
4. She was buried by the road.

FOUR THINGS GRANDPA JACOB DID FOR THEM

When it came to blessing the children, Jacob said many things to them; but words sometimes are not enough. There must be deeds to backup your words. So, Grandpa Jacob did four things for his grandsons.

1. *Grandpa Jacob adopted them.* When Jacob asked to see the boys, he made a very bold statement. The boys were half Hebrew and half Egyptians, but Jacob looked beyond their Egyptian nature, he wanted the boys to have the spiritual inheritance of Israel. So, Jacob said, "And now your two sons, Ephraim and Manasseh...are mine" (Gen. 48:5). This would have been astonishing to those who heard Jacob, for this was the language of adoption. Many families would have put a full-blooded Hebrew child far beyond a half-breed youth. But not Jacob. The love of Jacob in his heart for these two boys transcends normal tribal prejudice. He made a legal pronouncement to adopt Ephraim and Manasseh.

2. *Grandpa Jacob kissed and hugged them.* It was important in the Jewish economy to show affection to the children. But a "blessing" was more than showing affection, it was reflected in Jacob's heart overflowing for these boys to carry out his inheritance. "He kissed and embraced them" (Gen. 48:10).

When blessing a grandchild, you must do more than just say words over them. You pour your soul into them, and how do you do that? Your soul is transferred by the love you show them. When you kiss a child, embrace a child, and let him know that you love him; you're doing more than an outward physical symbol. You're putting your life into their life. This is similar to what Paul said to the Thessalonians, "You received not just the Word of God from us, but it was the Word of God in our hearts that was poured into your life, effectually making you what you are in Christ" (1 Thess. 2:13, author's translation).

3. *Grandpa Jacob laid his hands on them.* The blessing of grandparents must be transferred to their grandchildren, how can it be done? Remember, God likes symbols. He loves the symbol in the Lord's Table of the broken body and the spilt blood, just as He loves the symbols of the cross and the symbol of steeples that symbolically point the way to God. So when you bless a child, place your hands on his or her head, symbolizing your approval of the child, as well as a picture of your life flowing into theirs, "Then Israel stretched out his right hand and laid it on Ephraim's head, who was the younger, and his left hand on Manasseh's head, guiding his hands knowingly, for Manasseh was the firstborn" (Gen. 48:14). Jacob knew what he was doing, he was following the law that God had applied in his own life, i.e., *the oldest shall serve the youngest.* Jacob was blessing Ephraim—the second born—with the birthright of the family. Jacob was giving Ephraim the responsibility of spiritual leadership and intercession for the family. Even though Joseph protested, Jacob was led of God to bless Ephraim. Why? Because God saw that the future children of Ephraim would be leaders among the twelve tribes of Israel.

4. *Grandpa Jacob blessed his grandchildren.* The New Testament Hall of Fame says, "By faith Jacob, when he was dying, blessed each of the sons of Joseph" (Heb. 11:21). At that time, there was no Levitical blessing to give to the sons, however when a grandparent today is blessing his grandchild, he can use the Levitical blessing.

THE LEVITICAL BLESSING

"The Lord bless you and keep you; The Lord make His face shine upon you, and be gracious to you; The Lord lift up His countenance upon you, and give you peace" (Num. 6:24-26).

It's important for grandparents to bless their grandchildren. This is done in different ways, at different times, and for different purposes. Do it with boldness, however, some grandparents do it reluctantly. If the grandparent is reticent, children are sensitive; they will recognize their fearfulness, and the blessing may lose its meaning.

What should you do to bless your grandchildren? The following outline may give you some insight. (1) Pray and ask God to prepare you and help you. (2) Pray and ask God to prepare your grandchildren to receive the blessing. (3) Pray and ask God to give you the words to pray. (4) Find a meaningful reference in your Bible, highlight it for them to see, and/or write the reference on a separate sheet of paper. Be ready to share Bible verses with your grandchildren. (5) Do more than bless spiritually, make sure your grandchildren know what you plan to do for them in support of God's will for their life, how you will plan for them materially, and what you will do for them financially. (6) Make sure that you place special value on your grandchildren long before the actual event of blessing them; and long after you have blessed them. You placing hands on their head is not enough, your lifestyle must be a blessing to them. A blessing is *both* a long-term attitude of blessing, as well as a singular event of blessing. (7) Grandparents must not just wait for the grandchild to carry out the blessing in their life; a grandparent must make an active commitment to fulfill the blessing in the life of their grandchildren in every way possible. Grandparents must give their grandchildren time, counsel, example, and money.

HOW TO BLESS CHILDREN

1. A meaningful touch.
2. Blessing with a spoken word.
3. Attach high value to the one being blessed.
4. Picture of special future for the one being blessed.
5. An active commitment to fulfill the blessing

(From *God Bless You*, Elmer Towns, Regal Books, 2003)

FOUR THINGS GRANDPA JACOB GAVE THEM

This could have been an embarrassing situation. Jacob didn't have money or material resources to give to the grandsons, as did their father Joseph. Jacob didn't have time or strength; he had nothing to give but the blessing of God. So, what did Grandpa Jacob give to them?

1. *Grandpa Jacob gave them his name.* When Jacob adopted the two boys and brought them into the family line, he made them a part of his inheritance. Notice what he said, "Let my name be named upon them, and the name of my fathers Abraham and Isaac" (Gen. 48:16). When Jacob said before everyone, "They are mine" (Gen. 48:5), the boys legally became a part of his family.

It's important that your grandchildren know they belong to you, that they have a "special" connection to you. You are not their parents, so you cannot do everything that their parents do. Nor are you an aunt or an uncle. You are their grandparent, and you have a grandparent responsibility. What is that responsibility?

(1) You must accept them fully, without hesitation or qualification. (2) You must recognize that they have your blood flowing in their veins. (3) You must recognize that none

of your grandchildren are second-class family members. (4) You must love each equally, apart from time and circumstances. (5) You must give yourself to them as time and circumstances permit.

2. *Grandpa Jacob gave God's future to them.* God is the greatest thing that you can give to a child. You have given them the greatest thing in life when you give them knowledge of the Lord, and access to the Lord, and the promises of the Lord, and a vision of the Lord.

Jacob told his grandsons about the future. He said, "let them grow into a multitude in the midst of the earth" (Gen. 48:16). And then Jacob gave them the following, "So he blessed them that day, saying, "By you Israel will bless... And thus he set Ephraim before Manasseh" (Gen. 48:20).

3. *Grandpa Jacob gave them his love.* When you give a child your love, it's much more than giving a hug and a kiss. Love is opening up your heart to give yourself to the one you love. Isn't that what God did for us? "He loved us and sent His Son to be the propitiation for our sins" (1 John 4:10). There was nothing more that God could give to us than His Son, and there's nothing more that we can share with your grandchildren than God's Son.

4. *Grandpa Jacob gave them an example of worship.* Apparently, Jacob was sitting on a bed, i.e., an Egyptian bed. This was probably not a bed raised off the floor like Americans' sleep in. Jacob's bed was probably lying on a heavy blanket on the floor, similar to our spreading out a sleeping bag on the floor.

Jacob worshipped in two ways. First, "He bowed down with his face to the earth" (Gen. 48:12). He didn't have to get out of bed. He just got up on his elbows and knees to worship. Jacob thanked God for the opportunity of passing his spiritual inheritance on to his children. Then Jacob must have propped himself up, using his shepherd's staff for support. As he leaned on his staff, Jacob blessed his grandchildren.

a. *Jacob's position of worship.* Even though many were watching Jacob, he was more concerned with God, than with what people thought. "He bowed down with his face to the earth" (Gen. 48:12). When one prostrates oneself before God, it's because God is everything, and we offer ourselves to Him in service. This was Jacob's heart position.

b. *Jacob's attitude of blessing.* The Christian Hall of Fame describes, "When he was dying…leaning upon the top of his staff" (Heb. 11:21). Jacob must have propped himself up with his shepherd's staff, as he blessed the boys. Because of his advanced age, he might not have been able to support himself on his knees, so he propped himself on his staff.

LESSONS TO TAKE AWAY

1. *Grandparents should be concerned about the spiritual condition of their grandchildren.* Jacob didn't let pressure divert him away from his main goal, i.e., imparting spiritual blessing to his grandchildren. Every grandparent must have such a deep commitment to God that they will not let anything get in their way of communicating their faith to their grandchildren. Your passion is more important than any technique you use to influence them. Your heart is more important than any method you use, such as a phone call, a note, or cooking them a meal. Grandparents should be deeply concerned about the spiritual condition of their grandchildren.

2. *Grandparents should be spiritual examples.* What image do your grandchildren have of you? What do they think, and what do they remember? Sometimes words are forgotten, but good deeds that bless the children are always remembered. Therefore, be a great example to your grandchildren.

We (Ruth and Elmer) have been teaching in Christian colleges for almost fifty years. Over the years, we've noted a great change in the attitude toward the grandparents of young people who come to Christian colleges. During the '50s to '70s, we don't remember Christian young people saying a lot about their grandparents. There may have been conditional reasons why young people during that time didn't talk about their grandparents as much. However, in the '80s and '90s we've noticed the Christian young people often speak with deep appreciation of their grandparents. Christian young people share prayer requests of their grandparents' physical needs and take time off in school to attend grandparents' wedding anniversaries, family reunions, and even going home to visit grandparents when they're in the hospital. Young people didn't seem to be that concerned about their grandparents fifty years ago. What's the difference? As more mothers have gone back to work, the entire family has less time to spend on children. Mothers who work forty hours a week in secular employment, still have all their jobs around the house when they come home. As a result, children receive less time from their parents. True, parents today do a lot with their young people in sports teams and different clubs, but parents don't have time to just sit around talking, listening, and counseling. It's the grandparents who have more time than anyone else, they listen better than anyone else, and grandparents can mentor because they understand more about life than anyone else.

Also, grandparents are more forgiving than parents. Why? Because parents are responsible for the discipline and good behavior of their kids; but grandparents can overlook their failures and disobedience and love them anyway. *Go ahead and eat your dessert before dinner. Want another cookie?*

3. *Grandparents should give their testimony.* One of the best ways to make sure your grandchildren live for God is to tell them how you did it. When you share your victories and defeats, grandchildren will listen, and remember. They like stories, so tell them your life story. Tell them how you came to know Christ, how your life was changed, and what God has done for you through all of your years. Do you know the greatest answer to prayer you've ever had? Yes, you probably know; but do your grandchildren know? What's the greatest insight you've gotten from the Bible? What's the greatest way God has used you in Christian ministry? What's the greatest Christian friend you've ever had? You know these things, but do your grandchildren? They won't unless you tell them.

4. *Grandparents should bless their grandchildren both naturally and supernaturally.* There are so many ways that grandparents can bless naturally, i.e., by taking them for a hamburger, going to the amusement park, or coaching them about life skills, such as woodworking, hobbies, cooking, repairing an engine, or the vast other skills that grandparents have learned in their lifetime. Pass that on to your children naturally, and you bless them naturally.

But don't forget that you bless them spiritually when you coach them concerning the spiritual things you know. You know how to use a concordance to find verses in the Bible, but do your grandchildren? You know how to answer questions about the existence of God. What is the will of God? How can they know you're saved? And what attitudes and actions does God not want them to do? You'll bless your grandchildren spiritually when you give them that information.

To bless your grandchildren takes intention. You must plan to bless them. Make an appointment to be with them and bless them. Be intentional in carrying out the blessing. Why? Because there's an enemy who wants the souls of your grandchildren. He will steal the Word of God from their hearts if you let him. He will steal spiritual convictions from their heart if you let him; so plan to bless your grandchildren spiritually.

Chapter Three

NAOMI: GRANDMOTHER OF OBED

A COMPROMISING MOTHER BECOMES AN INFLUENTIAL GRANDMOTHER

Grandmother – Naomi

Mother – Ruth

Grandson – Obed

"So Boaz took Ruth and she became his wife; and when he went in to her, the LORD gave her conception, and she bore a son. Then the women said to Naomi, 'Blessed be the LORD, who has not left you this day without a close relative; and may his name be famous in Israel! And may he be to you a restorer of life and a nourisher of your old age; for your daughter-in-law, who loves you, who is better to you than seven sons, has borne him.' Then Naomi took the child and laid him on her bosom, and became a nurse to him. Also the neighbor women gave him a name, saying, 'There is a son born to Naomi.' And they called his name Obed. He is the father of Jesse, the father of David" (Ruth 4:13-17).

THE little boy stopped at the back door to smile at his grandmother, Naomi. The boy had been playing in the clay at the backwash table. He had made walls—like the walls of a city—and now his "make belief" city was drying in the sun. His little hands were not yet skilled, so the little city was crude.

"Look," he said to his grandmother, "I made a city." And with that, the little boy stepped on the wall and said, "Like God crushed the walls of Jericho." Then the boy asked his grandmother to tell the story again.

Naomi gave little Obed a cup of milk and set him at the table. Then Naomi told how his great-grandmother Rahab had lived in Jericho. She told how Rahab lived on the top of the wall in a small inn. There, travelers stayed the night.

Naomi told young Obed how generations ago God planned to destroy Jericho, but first two of God's servants came to spy out Jericho. They rented rooms in the small inn, and when the spies realized that Rahab and her family trusted in Jehovah, the spies told them what God was going to do. "God will destroy the city of Jericho," the spies told the family. (Rahab was formerly a sinful woman).

"But we believe in Jehovah," Rahab told the spies. It was then that the two spies told Rahab that if she would hang a long red rope out of her window, that she and her family would be saved when the Israeli army attacked Jericho. Grandma Naomi told how the priests marched around Jericho once a day. They carried the Ark of the Covenant—the presence of God—around the city once a day for seven days, and then on the seventh day, they marched around the city seven times.

"KABOOM!" Grandma Naomi made a big noise to tell her young grandson how God brought down the walls of Jericho. Then she reminded, "God saved Rahab and her family."

"Rahab was your great-grandmother," Naomi explained to the young kid who seemed to understand.

Rahab married one of God's servants, and they had a child named Boaz. "The little baby Boaz was your father," Grandma Naomi's high-pitched voice got young Obed excited.

Then Grandma Naomi began to share her story, telling about a famine that came to Bethlehem. "See these rich grain fields," Grandma Naomi pointed out the door toward Boaz's wheat fields. "Long ago they were dry, nothing would grow, and everything died."

"How did you eat," the young Obed asked grandmother. "We moved to the country of Moab," Naomi took the young boy to the door where she pointed. And miles away across a valley that was far away. "That's Moab." Naomi told how her husband and both of her sons died in Moab. "I thought I also would die in Moab," she told her grandson. "But just before I starved, I decided to come back home to Bethlehem."

Then Naomi's face smiled. She told her young grandson about saying goodbye to everyone she knew in Moab. Everyone left her but Ruth wanted to come with her to Bethlehem. Naomi explained, "Your mother wanted to come with me because she believed in Jehovah."

"Your mother and I didn't have anything to eat when we got here, so your mother went into the grain fields to pick up any food she could find. She just happened to go to one of your fathers' fields. When your father and your mother saw each other, it was love at first sight." Naomi told how Boaz flirted with Ruth. Grandma Naomi explained, "Your father invited your mother Ruth to come eat from his food basket, then he told all of the workers to drop grain right in front of your mother. You know what? Your mother got more grain than anybody else that day."

Little Obed laughed. He liked the part about his mother bringing home a whole sack full of grain.

"You were their first baby," Grandma Naomi explained to the little boy, "and I get to take care of you."

"Tell me how I got my name," the little boy begged, "please tell me the story again."

Grandma Naomi told how a baby is named when he is eight days old. "Your father wanted to call him after himself, i.e., Boaz, and your mother had a different name; but all the women at the village said, 'No!!' they wouldn't hear of it. The women said that everybody praised God because you were such a beautiful baby boy that was born to Boaz and Ruth. You were in the line of Messiah." Then Naomi said, "One day Messiah will come through you, he will be born of our family." Naomi explained that because the women praised and worshipped God so much, that, "You were called Obed, which means worship of the Lord."

"But that's not all," the little boy reminded his grandmother.

"Yes" she smiled in agreement with the little boy. "Obed also means servant; you are a servant who will bring worship to the Lord."

HOW NAOMI COMPROMISED

Lessons to Take Away

A parent can do a terrible job raising their children, but the Lord (the God of the second chance) can give them a second opportunity to do it right with grandchildren.

Naomi must have been quite a woman in her day. She and her husband were called "Ephrathites of Bethlehem." A phrase which means they were *bluebloods* or *upper class* or in our day, "the rich and famous." Technically the term *ephrathites* meant they were the original families of Bethlehem.

Naomi came from Bethlehem, a city which meant *House of Bread*, but after she got married it was anything but a house of bread. Fields turned brown, trees dropped their leaves, and nothing grew. The Bible says, "there was a famine in the land" (Ruth 1:1).

When difficult times come, people of character tighten their belts and with true grit they may get through difficult days. But not Naomi and her husband Elimelech. From Bethlehem you can look miles across the Dead Sea Valley and see Moab in the cloudy distance. They saw the green fields of Moab in stark contrast to the famine around them. Was it greed that motivated them to go to Moab, was it a search of a better life, maybe it was an excuse like many modern families, "I'm doing it for my family who needs the best of everything?"

WHAT DID NAOMI LEAVE?

- She left the land of promise for a land of compromise.
- She left the Temple in Jerusalem for a land of idols.
- She left the fellowship of God's people for unsaved heathen.
- She ran away from her problem, seeking an easy life.

When Naomi and Elimelech went to Moab, at first they just "went to sojourn" (Ruth 1:1), which means they were going to ride out the agricultural storm in Moab. They were probably planning on returning home.

But they didn't return home. Elimelech died in Moab. Was it God's punishment for compromise? Strange, Elimelech went to Moab to keep from dying, but it was there he died. Isn't that like people who don't want to give up anything for the Lord, yet they end up losing what they can't keep because they won't surrender to the Lord? Perhaps the problem is not that they settled down in Moab, but rather Moab settled down in them. The Bible says, "They went to the country of Moab and remained there" (Ruth

1:2). Maybe conditions were easier in Moab, and all they could remember about the Promised Land was famine. Remember it's not always easy to remain in the center of God's will, sometimes it's extremely difficult to remain in God's presence.

Next, the two sons married heathen women. Mahlon married Orpah, and Chilion married Ruth. The Bible doesn't mention any children, even though they were married for ten years. So without a husband, Naomi remained in Moab for a decade, no purpose, no plans, and no hope. She was waiting for the children that her two sons would give her; but children didn't come. Then Mahlon died and shortly thereafter Chilion died. Now you have three widows—three desperate women—without husband, without money, and without hope in the future.

Naomi compromised her commitment to the Lord. Naomi decides to return to the Promised Land, what else can she do? It seems her decision was made in desperation, rather than a spiritual commitment to God. Her two daughters-in-law decided to return with her, but Naomi discouraged them. "Go, return each to her mother's house. The Lord deal kindly with you, as you have dealt with the dead and with me" (Ruth 1:8). This seemed to be Naomi's honest desire for the two widows to have a remaining life. But then Naomi makes a tragic blunder.

Orpah started back to her family, but Ruth decided not to go. Ruth decided to stay with Naomi. It's then that Naomi says, "Look, your sister-in-law has gone back to her people and to her gods; return after your sister-in-law" (Ruth 1:15). Naomi wanted Ruth to return to her family and her heathen gods. But Ruth displayed faith in Jehovah. In this tragic moment of choice, Ruth made a decision that revealed her deep faith in God.

"Entreat me not to leave you, or to turn back from following after you; for wherever you go, I will go; and wherever you lodge, I will lodge; your people shall be my people, and your God, my God. Where you die, I will die, and there

will I be buried. The Lord do so to me, and more also, if anything but death parts you and me" (Ruth 1:16, 17).

Naomi compromised her family's influence. After her husband died, her sons were old enough to marry, and they chose Moabitess women. As a Jewish mother, Naomi knew that inter-marriage was wrong. If Naomi protested the Bible is silent, if she did anything to try to keep her sons from marrying outside the faith, again the Bible is silent. The only conclusion is that Naomi compromised her influence over her sons.

NAOMI'S COMPROMISE

Wrong place	went to Moab
Wrong priority	money
Wrong tolerance	tolerated Moab culture
Wrong counsel	sent Ruth back to her old life and gods

Naomi criticized God's provision for her. When Naomi came back to the Promised Land with Ruth, it was not a triumphant entry. Rather, Naomi came back with a critical spirit, "I went out full, and the LORD has brought me home again empty" (Ruth 1:21).

If Naomi died in Moab, her empty life would have had little notice. You would write *PRODIGAL* on her tombstone and add a postscript that it was good she came home at last. But in the next few years, Naomi redeemed her lost years, and made a contribution for God that has eternal positive consequences. She guided her daughter-in-law Ruth to marry Boaz, and from that came the line of King David and Jesus the Messiah.

NAOMI'S REPENTANCE SEEN IN HER ACTIONS

Naomi recognized God's punishment. When Naomi went to Moab, she didn't see God's STOP sign. Rather, she walked out of the center of God's will into a heathen culture belittling God for eternal consequences. Her husband died. Even then it didn't seem that Naomi realized the unfolding plan of God in her life. Only when she makes a decision to return to "The House of Bread" did she gain some spiritual insight into her past life. It's then she says, "The Lord has caused me to suffer and the Almighty has sent such tragedy" (Ruth 1:21, NLB).

Naomi guided Ruth toward her family heritage. When the women became desperate for food, Ruth assumed the position of a servant. She went out into the fields with other women to gather the sheaves that were missed by the harvesters. In Israel there was no such thing as welfare (Deut. 24:19; Lev. 19:9), but the law provided that the poor could work in the fields behind the harvesters. They could keep what they picked up. Thus, Ruth was living on welfare.

God makes big things happen through little details. And as Ruth went out to look for a place to work, the Bible says she "happened" on Boaz's field. When the Bible says he was, "A man of great wealth, of the family of Elimelech" (Ruth 2:1), it suggests that Boaz belonged to the same clan as Naomi's dead husband. They were related, but Ruth didn't know it.

Not only was Boaz a mighty landowner, he was a godly man. And when Boaz came into the field, he greeted his workers, "The Lord be with you!" and they answered him, "The Lord bless you!" (Ruth 2:4).

There was a law in Israel called the Kinsman Redeemer. It was described as a levirate marriage, which required a man to marry the widow of his deceased brother to raise up the family name (Deut. 25:5; Matt. 22:23-28). The fact that he was called a "Kinsman," the Hebrew word is *goel*, indicates the man was able to buy Ruth and Naomi out of bankruptcy and/or bondage. He could pay off their debt and set them free; but at the same time marry his dead relative's widow and reestablish the family line.

Interesting things happened in the barley field. Ruth worked hard but when Boaz arrived, she caught his eye. He asked the question, "Whose young woman is this?" Probably, Boaz was in his forties while Ruth was in her late twenties.

The workers told Boaz how hard Ruth had worked all morning. It was then that Boaz invited her to eat lunch with his workers, taking some of their bread and dipping it in the sauce. She also is able to eat the cooked grain and drink from the water jug reserved for the workers.

Boaz wanted to keep her around, so he said, "Do not go to glean in another field, nor go from here, but stay close by my young women" (Ruth 2:8). It's then that Boaz told his workers to drop extra sheaves for Ruth to glean. Boaz was "smitten."

When Ruth got home that evening, she had much more grain than Naomi expected. As a matter of fact, Ruth had more grain than any of the other gleaners. Naomi was surprised and asked where she had been working. It's then that Ruth answered, "The man's name with whom I worked today is Boaz" (Ruth 2:19).

It's then that Naomi recognized the name Boaz. He was her relative, and now Naomi who had no purpose, has a purpose. She who had no hope, has a captivating hope. Naomi was going to make sure Boaz married Ruth.

Naomi directed Ruth toward family and spiritual redemption. The wise Naomi directed Ruth, telling her how to go to the threshing floor where Boaz would be separating the kernels of grain from their chaff. Boaz would work hard all day, but Ruth was to go there under the cover of darkness. While some people want to suggest Ruth was immoral in going to Boaz at night, nothing happened immoral. When Boaz laid down to sleep, Ruth came and slept at his feet, such as a servant would sleep. One of the main reasons was for protection and the other, to keep the master's feet warm. After all, a man sleeps better if his feet are warm.

In the middle of the night Boaz was awakened and realized a woman was lying at his feet. When he found out it was Ruth, she didn't wait for him to propose marriage, rather she asked him to perform his family duty to buy her and Naomi out of bankruptcy. She said, "Take your maidservant under your wing, for you are a close relative (i.e., *goel*)" (Ruth 3:9).

After agreeing to redeem Naomi and Ruth, Boaz sent Ruth home with a sack full of grain. What man doesn't like to buy things for his sweetheart?

Naomi counseled Ruth to have patience and trust. You can imagine the next morning how Ruth and Naomi sat around the house wondering what would happen. It was then that wise Naomi said, "Sit still, my daughter...for the man will not rest until he has concluded the matter this day" (Ruth 3:18).

THE BLESSING ON GRANDMOTHER NAOMI

Boaz went to sit in the gate, which is a phrase meaning he went to the place where business negotiations were made in the city. It was there that he negotiated to buy the property that had belonged to Elimelech and Naomi; i.e., buying it out of bankruptcy. And with the property came the obligation for Boaz to marry Ruth and raise up the family line.

After Boaz and Ruth were married, God gave them the birth of a son. The women of the community became so excited about this blessed event that they recognized the world that Naomi had had and bring it about. The women praised the Lord

and insisted that the young baby Obed "would be famous in Israel." Obed means worshipper, the name is derived from a Hebrew word *ebed*, meaning a servant. The young child would be a servant of the Lord who worshipped the Lord.

"Then the women said to Naomi, 'Blessed be the Lord, who has not left you this day without a close relative; and may his name be famous in Israel! And may he be to you a restorer of life and a nourisher of your old age; for your daughter-in-law, who loves you, who is better to you than seven sons, has borne him'" (Ruth 4:14, 15).

1. *Grandma Naomi is given more importance in the life of Obed than the mother Ruth.* Notice how the women came to bless Naomi (Ruth 4:14), and recognize the child is "kin" to Naomi. Naomi becomes the primary caregiver when the Bible says that, "Naomi took the child and laid him on her bosom and became a nurse to him" (Ruth 4:16). This does not refer to her actually feeding the child, which would have been impossible at Naomi's age. It probably means she was the primary caregiver for Obed, charged with teaching, feeding, and teaching life-skills to the young child.

Ruth would have been busy as the manager of a large household, which included servants in the home as well as in the field. Therefore, Ruth needed the help of Naomi in raising Obed.

But it also showed the closeness between a wife and her mother-in-law. Traditionally, there is some tension, both women vying for the close affection between the one man in their lives, i.e., the husband on the part of the wife and the son on the part of the mother. But here both women demonstrate love, just as they had previously shared Naomi's son, now they share Ruth's son.

2. *The child is identified with his grandmother, rather than his father or his mother.* This is an unusual passage, for most sons are identified with their father. But there had been such a transformation in Naomi, that she received the attention in the Bible text (Ruth 4:14-17). Notice what they said, "There is a son born to Naomi" (Ruth 4:17). Even though Ruth was the birth mother, Naomi became the influential mother.

3. *The child Obed would become famous in Israel.* The word famous means, "name is proclaimed widely." And Obed became the great-grandfather of David. Perhaps the greatest name in Old Testament history was David, so Obed became famous for his great-grandson.

4. *The child gave grandmother Naomi a purpose in life.* When Naomi left for Moab, she became a compromiser. But when she returned to Bethlehem, she became a woman of conviction. What changed her? Sometimes hard times change a person. Other times, a *God encounter* changes a person. Still other times, people can change you. Perhaps it was the pure faith in Ruth that changed Naomi, because Ruth had a faith in God that Naomi lacked. This change in Naomi brought about her conviction.

Naomi came back to Bethlehem with no hope. She told Ruth, "Turn back, my daughters, go—for I am too old to have a husband. If I should say I have hope, if I should have a husband tonight and should also bear sons" (Ruth 1:12). You almost hear distress and resignation in her voice. But after Obed is born, she has new life. Notice what the Bible says, "May he (Obed) be to you a restorer of life" (Ruth 4:15).

When Naomi returned to the land, she had no spiritual energy, she had given up. She told her friends, "Call me Mara, for the Almighty had dealt very bitterly with me" (Ruth 1:20). But after Ruth bore a son, her life turned around. She was nourished. Again, notice what the Bible says, "May he be to you a...nourisher of your old age" (Ruth 4:15).

NAOMI'S NEW LIFE

The respect of the town's women	Ruth 4:14, 15
The love of her daughter-in-law	Ruth 4:15
Restoration of hope and vision	Ruth 4:15
A grandson in the Messianic line	Ruth 4:16

5. *Naomi gained the love of her daughter-in-law.* Whereas there's usually some tension between mother-in-law and daughter-in-law, there is no tension here. "Blessed be the Lord...your daughter-in-law, who loves you, who is better to you than seven sons" (Ruth 4:14, 15). Every woman wants a son, because a son will please her husband. But here Naomi is blessed with a daughter-in-law who is better than a son; no seven sons. Only God can give this type of love.

6. *Grandma Naomi had the responsibility of influencing Obed.* It appears that Naomi didn't do a good job raising her first son. She was a poor example taking him to Moab. She was a poor influence allowing her first son to marry outside the faith. But when given a second chance, she made sure that Obed was going to serve the Lord and worship Him. Even in the meaning of the name which young Obed assumed, this young boy would be faithful to God.

LESSONS TO TAKE AWAY

1. *A grandmother has accumulated both natural and spiritual wisdom, love, and understanding.* Because a grandmother has dealt with her children so many times, she has the wisdom and patience that's necessary with dealing with grandchildren. So, a grandmother can give better love...better counsel...and have more patience

with her grandchildren. Whereas Naomi did not do a good job with her children the first time around, her accumulated wisdom and spirituality were present to influence her grandson, Obed.

2. *Because grandparents have the advantage of seeing much of life, they should share as much as possible with their grandchildren.* Most grandparents have seen the *mean* side of life, and they want to spare their grandchildren difficulties. Also, grandparents have had many heartaches, and they want to protect their grandchildren from as much sorrows as possible. On the other side, grandparents have had victories and they have shouted, HALLELUJAH for answers to prayer. They should share all their experiences with their grandchildren. Can you see Obed's expression in Naomi's lap as she tells the young child about coming back to Bethlehem and having no food? Obed needed to hear how his mother worked hard in the fields to save "life and limb." Also, young Obed needed to know that his father provided a wonderful home for Ruth, his grandmother and for him.

3. *One of the greatest purposes when you reach retirement is to properly influence your grandchildren.* What is retirement for...shuffleboard... fishing...puttering around the house? While all these things are enjoyable, nothing is more eternal than investing your time and wisdom in a grandchild. I (Elmer) have often said that a man in ministry should not retire, because ministry is your life. Ministry is what you would rather do than anything else. However, for working people in a job that is demanding and that "saps your life," you should look forward to retirement and the good things of life. However, the best thing for all people in retirement is to make your grandchildren the focus of your life, and to pour your influence into them.

4. *Grandchildren give energy to grandparents.* Naomi had many experiences to share with Grandson Obed. Before she left Bethlehem for Moab, she was an Ephrodite, meaning a blue blood in the community. Because famine struck, she went to Moab where she was a foreigner and a minority. She had to go on welfare in Moab when her husband and two sons died. Naomi's next experience was as a returning prodigal where she and Ruth lived on Jewish welfare. Finally, when Naomi became a grandmother, she was elevated in the eyes of the women in the community and given a place of responsibility. It was here that the women said, "He shall be to you a restorer of life and a nourisher of your old age" (Ruth 4:15). Obed gave purpose to Naomi so that she had new energy in the sunset years of her life.

Today, your grandchildren can revitalize your life, because it will take all of your energy to entertain them while they visit your home. Your energy will be restored by their energy, because grandchildren will run through your house, play in every corner, and will be constantly active until they leave. Then you fall exhausted into a chair to recuperate.

What is the *second* most delightful thing in the life of grandparents? It's when they see their grandchildren coming up the walk for a visit. Then you ask, what's the *first* most delightful thing in the life of grandparents? It's when they see the grandchildren leave, and you're exhausted.

5. *A grandchild may give a second chance to a grandparent who messed up their child-rearing responsibilities the first time around.*

Naomi didn't do the job right the first time. She and her husband focused on money during the famine, so they left the Promised Land and went to Moab. She didn't do a good job directing her sons because they married foreigners, marrying outside their Jewish faith. Some grandparents think they will suffer consequences the rest of their life because they messed up their child-rearing opportunity. Perhaps they may have a prodigal child, or they may have neglected a child, but when a grandchild comes along, grandparents have a second opportunity to "set the record straight." Naomi was given an opportunity to influence Obed. "Naomi took the child and laid it at her bosom and became nurse to it" (Ruth 4:16).

Because Obed became the grandfather to David, we know that Obed must have been given good direction for his life; as was given to his son Jesse, and then to his grandson, King David.

6. *Grandparents see life's big picture, seeing a long way into the past, and a long way into the future.*

Naomi could look all the way back to Great Grandmother Rahab, who chose to follow the God of Israel. That was a wonderful story of grace that she could tell Obed. Then, Grandma Naomi could tell her *life-story* to Obed, explaining about the consequences of disobedience. Her past history became the basis for directing the future life of Obed.

Give the best of your life for the rest of your life.

When you get to be a grandparent, you usually have some accumulated money, and accumulated wisdom. You've been to many places, done many things, and learned from them all. Walking through some grandparents' homes, you see trinkets, souvenirs, and mementos. Those things represent travel experiences, vacations, and the many jobs they've experienced. Don't forget scrapbooks. Grandparents have pictures of their children when they were babies, as well as pictures of their grandchildren. So, realize that these pictures are more than just visual images, they represent the accumulated experiences of a life lived long, doing many different things and accomplishing many different goals. Now that you're a grandparent and have these experiences, share your life, because your grandchildren need the best of you. What should you do? *Give the best of your life, for the rest of your life.*

Chapter Four

ASA: GRANDSON OF MAACHAH

Overcoming An Evil Grandmother

Grandmother – Maachah

Father – Jehoram

Son – Asa

"Asa did what was right in the eyes of the LORD, as did his father David. And he banished the perverted persons from the land, and removed all the idols that his fathers had made. Also he removed Maachah his grandmother from being queen mother, because she had made an obscene image of Asherah. And Asa cut down her obscene image and burned it by the Brook Kidron" (1 Kings 15:11-13).

MY name is Asa, I was born the year that my great grandfather King Solomon died. When I was a baby the palace was gloriously rich, and all the guards had golden shields. All the utensils on the dining table were gold. I heard talk from the servants and my cousins about the "Golden Days" when Solomon was King. I knew one day I would be king, and I wanted everything to be as glorious as Solomon's reign when I became king.

But things did not go well when I was growing up. I remember that frightful time when Egyptian soldiers surrounded the walls of Jerusalem and threatened to kill us all. I was five years old and had terrible nightmares. My Grandpa Rehoboam gave the Egyptians all the gold to make their soldiers go away. He gave them the gold from the treasury, the gold cups of the table, and the gold shields of the soldiers. Everyone was very sad, but I kept thinking, "When I get to be king, it'll be glorious."

Things continued to get worse under Grandpa Rehoboam. There was no money, and he lost over half the kingdom—ten Northern Tribes—but he kept Solomon's Temple and Jerusalem. My Grandma Maachah was always complaining about having to go to the Temple to worship Jehovah. She fussed about the Ten Commandments, but I kept thinking, "I'll obey Jehovah when I get to be king." Grandpa Rehoboam worshipped foreign idols because he thought they'd protect him and make him rich. Grandmother Maachah loved the idols even more. I'll worship Jehovah when I become king.

When I was seventeen years old, Grandpa Rehoboam died, and I thought things would get better when my father Abijah became king. But my father was a weak king. Grandma Maachah told my father Abijah what to do, just as she told Grandpa Rehoboam what to do, and they obeyed her. Grandmother Maachah said the people wanted to worship idols, so father built temples to Baal. But Grandma Maachah didn't just want idols, she wanted a woman-god. She built a great image to Asherah, the Canaanite mother goddess. She placed it in a grove of trees outside her apartment and burned incense there. I knew this was wrong. When I become king, I'll get rid of all the heathen idols.

My father Abijah didn't rule righteously, he let money go to his head, and he married many wives. He didn't please God. Within two years he died, and I became king when I was only 21 years old. I knew

to have a glorious kingdom I'd have to get rid of idols and sin.

The first thing I did was to put Grandmother Maachah out of the palace and take away her crown. She would no longer be the queen mother. I broke her female idol into rubble and dumped it into a surrounding valley. I went into my father's house and destroyed all the idols that my father worshipped. Then I got rid of all of the Sodomites in the Baal temple and destroyed the temple itself.

I am going to be a godly king; I'll rule righteously for God. I want God's kingdom to be glorious again.

MAACHAH, AN UNGODLY GRANDMOTHER

Lessons to Take Away

Extreme abuses in grandparents can lead to the opposite reaction in grandchildren, i.e., that godly grandchildren can come from ungodly grandparents.

Let's look at Grandma Maachah; what kind of woman was she? When Grandpa Rehoboam married Grandma Maachah, he had no idea what kind of a wife she would be. Rebellious Maachah was the daughter of Absalom, the rebellious son of David who tried to steal the kingdom from David. Rebellious Absalom never lived by the rules; he made his own rules. Absalom never submitted to his father's rule, he wanted to rule over his father, David. He was a power-driven young man, and his daughter, Maachah, too was power-driven.

Absalom murdered his brother Amnon. It was not a murder of rage, but Absalom cruelly planned the murder and killed his brother. When his daughter

Maachah married King Rehoboam, she too got rid of anyone in her way just like her father.

Absalom pretended to be loyal to his father, and smiled to his face, but behind his father's back, he was treacherous and turned people against David. When finally, Absalom tried to kill David, one of David's generals had to kill Absalom.

So, when Grandma Maachah married Rehoboam, what chance did Asa's grandfather have to become a godly man? None! Maachah was a vindictive, mean-spirited woman who would break every law—including God's law—to get her way. Maachah influenced her husband to evil, then she did the same thing to her son. "Now Rehoboam loved Maachah the daughter of Absalom more than all his wives and his concubines...and Rehoboam appointed Abijah the son of Maachah as chief, to be leader among his brothers; for he intended to make him king" (2 Chron. 11:21, 22).

Like father, like son. Now let's see what kind of man Grandpa Rehoboam was. Solomon was the wisest man on earth, and most people thought his son Rehoboam would be equally smart. But just as Solomon was betrayed by women, so Solomon's son Rehoboam was betrayed by a woman, i.e., Maachah. Rehoboam was weak-willed, indecisive and couldn't be trusted to make the right decisions for God. Rehoboam wouldn't listen to the wise counsel of the elderly men who wanted young Rehoboam to reduce taxation on the people. The elders wanted Rehoboam to rule by love, not by force. But Rehoboam listened to his young hotheaded friends; he increased the taxes and the people rebelled. That's when Rehoboam lost the ten northern tribes into a separate nation.

Where was Maachah when this split occurred? Rather than counseling her husband to wisdom, the rebellious Maachah pushed her husband to rebel against the people he ruled.

Rehoboam's continuing sin corrupted the kingdom. Seldom do rebellious people learn wisdom and self-control, and Maachah continued to push her husband into a downward spiral of sin. "And he (Rehoboam) did evil, because he did not prepare his heart to seek the Lord" (2 Chron. 12:14).

Grandma Maachah gave her son an evil name. The son that was to be the next king of Israel had two names. His first name was Abijah, which means, "The Lord is my Father." That might have been the name that Rehoboam called his son to satisfy the religious nature of the people. But Maachah gave him an evil name, she called him Abijam, which means, "My father is Yam." She named him for a Canaanite god of the sea.

Maachah supported sexual Sodom. When Abijam built a temple for Baal, the priest also instituted male prostitutes as a form of worship. This is one of the filthiest heathen practices ever. Someone has said that if sexual sins were a train leading to destruction, the Caboose is homosexuality. When Asa became king, one of the first things he did was to get rid of the heathen temple, and the Sodomites. "And he banished the perverted persons from the land and removed all the idols that his fathers had made" (1 Kings 15:12).

Maachah worshipped false gods. She not only provided a temple that the people asked for, and idols that they wanted, she also worshipped female Canaanite gods. This is terrible because Maachah had the royal blood of David flowing in her veins. But when Asa became king, he "removed all the idols that his father and mother had made" (1 Kings 15:12, author's translation).

Maachah secretly had a sexual goddess-idol. The Hebrew language suggests that the idol that Maachah had made was a female idol, i.e., a female sex god. "And Asa cut down her obscene image and burned it by the Brook Kidron" (1 Kings 15:13). Idols are not just mere small statues made of wood or stone. Rather, when people worship something made of stone, they worship the spirit or power the stone represents. Because Baal represented fertility, when farmers wanted their livestock to prosper, they worshipped the god of fertility hoping their flocks would produce offspring. What spirit of fertility was that? It was more than animism, i.e., a worship of neutral spirits; it was worship of demon spirits. An idol represents a spirit-demon, suggesting Maachah who kept her secret female idol outside her window was utterly evil and controlled by Satan.

ASA, A GODLY GRANDSON

Extreme abuses lead to a radical reaction in some children. Grandpa Rehoboam sinned and started God's people down the path to evil. His son Abijah continued down that path. But a small boy growing up in the palace saw the abuses, and in his heart knew what was right. God was preparing Asa to be the first revival king of God's people. "Abijah walked in all the sins of his father, which he had done before him; his heart was not loyal to the LORD his God, as was the heart of his father David" (I Kings 15:3). When young Asa saw all that his father did, he determined to be different.

I (Elmer) grew up in a home with an alcoholic father. While my father was good and kind, all of our family's money went for liquor. When I saw problems in our house, not enough money for rent, food, and basic necessities of life; I determined as a young boy I was not going to be like my father. I determined I would not be a drunk. I determined as a young boy sitting in a Sunday school class that I would never take my first drop of alcohol. In my case, abuses in my father led to reaction in this son.

God sovereignly prepared Asa for his godly rule. Even though circumstances formed Asa's attitude toward life, sovereignly the Holy Spirit was preparing a young boy to rule God's people. "Nevertheless, for David's sake the LORD his God gave him a lamp

in Jerusalem, by setting up his son (Asa) after him and by establishing Jerusalem" (1 Kings 15:4).

Asa began with reforms, and later introduced revival. Almost immediately upon his coronation, Asa began cleansing the temple. Aren't twenty-one-year-old young men reactionary? Don't they act first and think afterward? Asa immediately began cleansing the nation. "He removed the altars of the foreign gods and the high places and broke down the sacred pillars and cut down the wooden images" (2 Chron. 14:3). You can almost hear the *whack* of the axe, and the *crunch* of the sledgehammer. Asa probably didn't stay back in the palace and let his military leaders carry out the job. Young King Asa was probably standing on the steps of the temple of Baal directing his soldiers to destroy the evil place.

Asa demanded righteousness in the nation. Young men think they can demand allegiance from followers, but it's only the wise man who knows that people follow from their hearts, not from the law. "He (Asa) commanded Judah to seek the LORD God of their fathers, and to observe the law and the commandment" (2 Chron. 14:4). Even if commanding the people to follow the Lord doesn't always work, wouldn't you rather have Asa prodding the people to godliness, rather than his Grandmother prodding them to lust after evil?

Asa raised and fortified the nation. Not only did Asa destroy the wicked infrastructures of the nation; the young king gave attention to military fortifications. "And he built fortified cities in Judah, for the land had rest; he had no war in those years, because the LORD had given him rest" (2 Chron. 14:6). It wasn't enough just to have stone walls for protection. "And Asa had an army of three hundred thousand from Judah...and from Benjamin two hundred and eighty thousand men" (2 Chron. 14:8). Asa raised a standing army of over a half million soldiers. With the forts and warriors, the nation had peace.

Asa's ultimate defense was in the Lord his God. When attacked, Asa didn't just depend upon his soldiers or high protective walls. When attacked, "Asa cried out to the Lord his God, and said, Lord, it is nothing for You to help, whether with many or with those who have no power; help us, O Lord our God, for we rest on You, and in Your name we go against this multitude. O Lord, You are our God; do not let man prevail against You!" (2 Chron. 14:11). Notice, he was not just defending his people and his nation, Asa was defending the Lord God. For he reminded God in his prayer that the enemy is attacking God Himself.

Asa led the nation in revival. Revival usually starts with a man or woman who is filled with the spirit of God, delivers the message of God. Azariah the prophet was that man that precipitated revival. "Now the Spirit of God came upon Azariah the son of Oded" (2 Chron. 15:1). This prophet Azariah went out to meet Asa to deliver unto him the message of God. "The Lord is with you while you are with Him. If you seek Him, He will be found by you; but if you forsake Him, He will forsake you" (2 Chron. 15:2).

Almost fifteen years after Asa, the reforming king assumed the crown, he became the revival king. At age 36, Asa introduced the ministry of the Word of God. "For a long time, Israel has been without the true God, without a teaching priest, and without law" (2 Chron. 15:3).

True, Asa had destroyed Baal's temple, but now he focused on the purpose of Solomon's Temple. What did Asa do? He, "restored the altar of the LORD that was before the vestibule of the Lord" (2 Chron. 15:8). When the altar was restored, it was not just for show. The altar was the place where the blood sacrifice was offered for the sins of the people. Now Asa reminded people to come with their blood sacrifice for the forgiveness of sins. He now emphasized the spiritual nature of their religion, i.e., the relationship between a man and his God.

Asa celebrated the feast of the Lord. Asa exhorted the people to come up to Jerusalem and celebrate the feast by worshipping the Lord. Did they come? Yes, "when they saw that the LORD his God was with him." (2 Chron. 15:9). As a result, people obeyed the Lord and worshipped at the feast. "So, they gathered together at Jerusalem in the third month, in the fifteenth year of the reign of Asa" (2 Chron. 15:10). And what did they do? "They offered to the Lord" (2 Chron. 15:11).

Asa led the people to renew their dedication to God. When the people came to Israel, it was not just enough to fill their heads with knowledge or stir their hearts with devotion. He pledged their hand to obedience. "They entered into a covenant to seek the LORD God of their fathers with all their heart and with all their soul" (2 Chron. 15:12). So, revival began when the people's hearts were right with God. "And all Judah rejoiced at the oath, for they had sworn with all their heart and sought Him with all their soul; and He was found by them, and the Lord gave them rest all around" (2 Chron. 15:15).

When the people entered into an oath with God, it was not because they were forced to obey God, as Asa had done when he first became king. This time the people willingly obeyed God and sought Him with their whole heart. "Then they took an oath before the LORD with a loud voice, with shouting and trumpets and rams' horns" (2 Chron. 15:14).

LESSONS TO TAKE AWAY

1. *The Law has its exception.* Some say, "Like father like son." But that's not always true. Some children grow up to be the opposite of their parents. Why do some children leave home walking in a different direction from their parents? Sometimes it's the influence of a godly man (King Josiah). Sometimes it's circumstances (Asa). Sometimes it's a death in the family (Mephibosheth). Sometimes the child identifies more with the loving nature of a mother, rather than the harsh nature of his father. Whatever the

reason, there are always exceptions to the law, "like produces like." Asa was not at all like his father and grandfather.

When Asa was a small child, "there no peace to the one who went out...but great turmoil... nation was destroyed by nation, and city by city" (2 Chron. 15:5, 6). This means that the land was lawless, people were mugged in the streets, and women were not safe. When Asa was a small boy, he had personal guards because he was the son of the king. But the average person put their life into their own hands when they ventured out beyond their city. When Asa was growing up, one city attacked another, and one nation attacked another. Young Asa saw lawlessness and danger everywhere and wanted a different world. He remembered the stories he heard around the dinner table about the reign of his great grandfather Solomon. Solomon did not have wars, but rather peace. That's what young Asa wanted. Peace!

2. *Sometimes the evil influence of parents produces children more evil than themselves.* This principle was seen in that Maachah was more evil than her father Absalom. While Absalom used guile and trickery in an attempt to gain the kingdom, Maachah used great force and ruthlessness. Both the father Absalom and the daughter Maachah were evil, but they expressed it in different ways. What can be seen from their life? That when Absalom was evil, Maachah was twice as evil.

3. *Sin is like a rotten animal under the house, its stench can't be covered.* Grandma Maachah was an evil woman who influenced her husband against worship of Jehovah God. She made him choose evil and was the ultimate cause for the corruption of his kingdom. Her evil was expressed in the idol she kept in her yard, i.e., a female goddess. She might have reasoned that if male prostitutes were worshipping in the temple Baal, why could she not have a female idol to tickle her fancy.

But her idol was known by her grandson Asa. And one of the first things he did when becoming king was to get rid of her, her influence, and her female goddess.

How did Asa know about the female idol? Surely there must have been servants who talked about the female goddess, and word spread through the palace where a teenage boy named Asa listened to groups of servants talk. When people are addicted to gross sin, it's hard to cover it up, and it's hard to keep it quiet.

4. *A family can be cursed to the third and fourth generation.* God had promised that when the head of the family goes bad, the sin will continue to the third and fourth generation. "I the Lord your God, am a jealous God, visiting the iniquity of the fathers upon the children to the third and fourth generations of those who hate Me" (Ex. 20:5). In Asa's case, iniquity extended only to the third generation, not the fourth. Notice it went from Absalom → Maachah → Abijah → Asa. Young King Asa was the fourth generation from Absalom, and he turned out righteous.

5. *God will sovereignly raise up righteous children.* Out of a prostitute's sin have come some great godly preachers. Out of the homes of Atheist have come great Bible teachers. Out of dens where people fight God, have come those who defend the name of God. "But where sin abounded, grace abounded much more" (Rom. 5:20). Technically the reference in Romans suggests that out of the disobedience of Adam and Eve, came the gift of eternal life through Jesus Christ who died for the sins of the world (Rom. 5:15-21). But this reference can also be applied to grandchildren. Where sin abounded in Rehoboam and Abijah, grace abounded much more in Asa.

6. *Sometimes the grandchild has to deal with the sins of the grandparent.* How hard was it for young twenty-one-year-old Asa to dispose his grandmother? Did he have difficulty dealing with her

sins? That's a question that can be difficult to answer. A child has natural love for his parents, so it's difficult to go against them. But at the same time the child who loves God, can obey God even more than parents. And a child's love of God can help him deal with the sins of his grandparents.

Jesus said, "If anyone comes to Me and does not hate his father and mother, wife and children, brothers and sisters, yes, and his own life also, he cannot be My disciple" (Luke 14:26). The word "hate" does not mean that you must turn your emotions against your parents when you follow Jesus Christ. That is not what Jesus meant. The word "hate" shows a comparison of two different worlds. You are to love God so much, and to follow Christ so devotedly, that in *comparison* your natural love to your parents will seem like hatred in light of your immense love to Jesus Christ.

7. *A grandchild can become godlier as he/she grows older.* Asa began his rule as a young man who reformed the nation. He was carrying out the dreams he had as a young child growing up in the palace. But when he met the man of God and was challenged with the Word of God; Asa responded to the next level in his spiritual growth. He took his *reforms* into *revivals*.

Asa began cleaning up his nation outwardly but ended up dealing with the hearts of the people inwardly. He wanted them to follow God with all of their hearts, so he had made them pledge a vow of commitment to seek God first and to follow Him with all their hearts.

Chapter Five

NOAH: GRANDFATHER TO CANAAN

WHEN GRANDPARENTS BECOME A STUMBLING BLOCK TO GRANDCHILDREN

Grandfather – Noah – *Sinned*

Father – Ham – *Gossiped*

Grandson – Canaan – *Laughed*

"And Noah began to be a farmer, and he planted a vineyard. Then he drank of the wine and was drunk, and became uncovered in his tent. And Ham, the father of Canaan, saw the nakedness of his father, and told his two brothers outside. But Shem and Japheth took a garment, laid it on both their shoulders, and went backward and covered the nakedness of their father. Their faces were turned away, and they did not see their father's nakedness. So, Noah awoke from his wine, and knew what his younger son had done to him. Then he said: Cursed be Canaan; a servant of servants he shall be to his brethren" (Genesis 9:20-25).

MY name is Noah and you all know me because I built the ark. And you know about the flood that covered the entire earth. But today I am not here to talk about the flood, I want to talk to you about my grandson Canaan. This is a difficult story to tell because all grandfathers have difficulty when their grandsons turn evil.

But there is another aspect of the story that embarrasses me. I got drunk and sinned and my sin hurt my grandson. Of all the people who should have known about drunkenness, it was me. Remember, for years I warned everyone that God was going to judge the world with a flood. No one would listen to me because people were giving themselves over to drunkenness, and sexual perversion. They were dabbling in demonism and worshiping Satan. I should have known what would happen to me when I got drunk because I saw what God did to the world; He judged them.

Before the flood, I was a carpenter, and a pretty good one at that. I built something that no one else had ever built in history. I built the biggest thing a man had ever built, 450 feet long, 3 stories tall, and 75 feet wide. I built a boat, just me and my three sons. In your day, that's as big as a large 3-story apartment building. And let me tell you how good my boat was, it didn't break up in 40 days of storms. It floated for an entire year, saving me and my wife, and three sons and their wives.

After the flood I gave up carpentry and went into farming. I grew all my food, and I especially enjoyed some sweet luscious grapes. Mm-m-m-m-m! They were mouth-watering good every time I put a grape in my mouth. One day after making sweet crushed grape juice, I absent-mindedly left a bucket of grape juice hanging on a peg in the storehouse. I didn't know what fermentation was, but the sweet grapes rotten and then fermented. Just as I was going to throw that bucket out, I smelled a different fragrance and decided to taste it. You know, it only takes one taste for a man to become an alcoholic. One drink led to another and before I knew what happened, I was drunk.

I only tasted a little at first, then got so drunk I passed out. That's when the terrible act occurred. I was drunk on the floor, naked and had passed out. My grandson Canaan came in and that's when the sin happened. God hates sin; it's so bad I can't describe it in public.

But my son Ham—that's Canaan's father—was horrified, but he didn't do anything. He could have covered me, but he didn't. The only thing he did was run to tell his brothers. My other two sons, Japheth and Shem, walked in backward with a sheet over their shoulders to cover me. I'm thankful for that.

Sometimes a man curses because he is mad; sometimes a man will even curse in God's name. But the cursing that took place that day was different. It wasn't just me cursing my grandson, it was God speaking through me. For God saw in Canaan a sexual weakness and lustful appetite. God knew that his sin would be perpetrated upon his children and passed on to their children, and they in turn would have the same influence on their children. So, I spoke God's curse upon Canaan,

"Cursed [be] Canaan; A servant of servants He shall be to his brethren" (Gen. 9:25).

I don't know what's going to happen to that boy, nor do I know what will happen to his succeeding generations. But I do know grandparents must be careful to live a godly life before their grandchildren. I also know the sin of grandparents can have disastrous consequences on their grandchildren.

WHAT HAPPENED THAT DAY?

Lessons to Take Away

Sin in the life of a grandparent can have a disastrous influence on grandchildren.

Wine is first mentioned in the Bible when Noah became a farmer, planted grapes, and eventually got drunk off of the fruit of his harvest. When Noah preached against sin before the flood, he probably included the sin of "drinking" (Matt. 24:38). Though Noah was guilty of the sin of drunkenness, carelessness, and being a negative role model, the sin of Canaan was much more serious. Canaan's sin revealed perhaps his suppressed carnal attitude toward sin, or his rebellious attitude toward his grandfather, and perhaps a resentment against God in Heaven.

When Noah awoke from his drunkenness, he spoke the words of a curse over his grandson Canaan, which were probably the words of God who knew the sins of Canaan's heart. God, who alone knows the future, looked down the hallway of time and knew that the grandson Canaan's sin toward Noah's nakedness would be carried out in the sexual sins of the Canaanite nations that lived in the Promised Land. When Joshua destroyed the Canaanites and drove them from the Promised Land, he carried out the curse of Noah against Canaan.

WHAT WE KNOW FOR SURE

Noah was godly. When the entire face of the earth was given over to sin, God could only find one righteous family, and through that family, God determined to save mankind. "Noah found grace in the eyes of the Lord...Noah was a just man and perfect in his generation, and Noah walked with God" (Gen. 6:8, 9).

Noah warned the world of coming judgment. God revealed to Noah that He was going to destroy the earth. "And the LORD said, My Spirit shall not strive with man forever, for he is indeed flesh" (Gen. 6:3). Why would God destroy them? "Then the Lord saw that the wickedness of man was great in the earth, and that every intent of the thoughts of his heart was only evil continually. And the Lord was sorry that He had made man on the earth, and He was grieved in His heart. So, the Lord said, I will destroy man whom I have created from the face of the earth, both man and beast, creeping thing and birds of the air, for I am sorry that I have made them" (Gen. 6:5-7).

God spoke to Noah—whether audibly or internally—warning him of the coming flood. "By faith Noah, being divinely warned of things not yet seen, moved with godly fear, prepared an ark...by which he condemned the world" (Heb. 11:7).

Originally Noah was a carpenter. His occupation before the flood was building things, probably the houses for the godly line of Seth. And then God said, "Make yourself an ark of gopherwood" (Gen. 6:14). This was no ordinary boat (the word ark means box). The ark was a large floating box (barge) 450 feet long, 75 feet wide, and 50 feet tall (three stories). Noah wasn't just a carpenter, he built massive things (the ark was as large as a large three-story tall college dormitory, that is longer than a football field). But Noah was an outstanding carpenter, for the ark he built was able to withstand the storms and torrential rainfall for forty days, and deliver the family safe for the one year they lived in the ark.

Noah was a preacher. The size of the ark was warning in itself to the world that a flood was coming. But more than a vessel of safety, this ark warned the unrighteous people of coming judgment. Noah also preached, "Noah...a preacher of righteousness" (2 Peter 2:5) and warned the people of coming judgment.

The sin of drunkenness. Probably drunkenness was not the primary sin of the generations before the flood. They were guilty of idolatry, sexual perversion, and other sins outlined in Romans 1:1-27 (this would have involved spirit worship, which was probably demon worship). Isn't most idol worship a recognition of the spirit behind the idol, which is usually a demon spirit?

Jesus likened the events prior to the flood to the events prior to his Second Coming to the earth. Jesus said, "But as the days of Noah were, so also will the coming of the Son of Man...drinking...until the day that Noah entered the ark" (Matt. 24:37, 38). The emphasis here is on drunkenness, because that is the sin of which Noah was guilty in his later life.

When judgment was ready. One week before God opened the heavens to bring forth rain on the earth, God called Noah and his family into the ark. The Lord said, "Come into the ark, you and all your household" (Gen. 7:1). At the time Noah was six hundred years old (Gen. 8:13). He had not had sons before he was five hundred years old, so his three sons were all under a hundred years old. However, don't compare a hundred-year-old man to our age today. In Noah's age, the body had probably not deteriorated from the accumulated germs and bacteria that infected humans after the Fall in the Garden of Eden. When God warned Adam, "Thou shalt surely die," the Hebrew language says literally, "And dying, thou shalt die." This means that death would be a gradual process, followed by a climactic event. Therefore, the gradual process of deterioration from bacteria did not yet reach its accumulative end in seventy years, that we experience today (Ps. 90:10).

After coming out of the ark, Noah and his family faced a clean new world. There was no sin in the world that they entered into, yet the seed of sin is born in the heart of every child; so, the root of sin

entered the new world as the children and grandchildren of Noah populated the face of the earth.

Noah's new occupation. After the flood, Noah changed his occupation from carpentry to farming. "Noah began to be a farmer, and he planted a vineyard" (Gen. 9:20). We cannot imagine that this godly man would purposely have fermented wine, and literally drank to destroy his example before his family, and became drunk to the spiritual destruction of a grandson named Canaan. Most believe that Noah stumbled on the process of fermentation, and once he tasted the "brew" it became addictive.

Alcohol is an addictive poison that will make slaves of some with only one taste, and after a lifetime of drunkenness will destroy your body and mind, loosen your self-discipline, turn friends and family against you, and destroy your character.

Noah's threefold sin. The sin was not in simply tasting the wine, but in the entire process that followed. "He (Noah) drank of the wine and was drunk, and became uncovered in his tent" (Gen. 9:21).

NOAH'S SIN

- Drunkenness—the sin he preached against
- Exposure—he uncovered himself, i.e., *Gulah* (Reflective)
- Destroyed his godly example

How did Noah know? After Noah awoke from his drunkenness, for some reason he knew what had happened. This is an interesting question that deserves some speculation.

- Revelation: God told Noah what happened
- Inquiry: He asked or was told what happened
- Memory: A drunk man remembers some things

WHAT WAS THE SIN OF HAM AND CANAAN?

Apparently, Canaan was the one who discovered his grandfather's nakedness, and did something—we don't know what—that reflected his evil heart. Some say he laughed at Noah, and his relationship to God. Some say it was a sexual act, i.e., a homosexual act. Some say it was something we don't know. In any occasion, Canaan told his father Ham what he saw. When Ham heard about it, he should have done something, i.e., he should have done what his older brothers did. Ham should have put a coat upon his shoulders and backing into the room covered his father's nakedness. But Ham didn't.

Ham told his older brothers about his father's nakedness. It was then that the two older brothers put a covering over their shoulders and backed into the room to cover their father's nakedness. When Noah awoke, he knew what had happened. It was then that God spoke a curse through Noah on Canaan, and his posterity.

Seeing only. The Bible doesn't say that Canaan saw the nakedness of his grandfather, but he was cursed; implying Canaan had done something worse than just looking at his grandfather. Ham just looked, "Ham, the father of Canaan, saw the nakedness of his father, and told his two brothers outside" (Gen. 9:22). What goes with the act of seeing? If Canaan just saw his grandfather's nakedness, why was he cursed, but his father Ham not cursed? The act of looking by Ham could be wrong. Why could the act of observing nudity be wrong?

- Lust
- Mockery
- Rejection of grandfather's spiritual authority
- Didn't cover his nakedness

From all that we can read throughout Scripture, just observing nakedness is not a sin serious enough to be condemned for the next generations.

Apparently, Canaan did something deeper or more serious. Whatever the deeper sin, it was serious enough to bring God's curse upon Canaan and all those in his biological line.

The two older sons—Shem and Japheth—did not go in to look at their father. This was more than not being curious; they were being respectful. What did they do? "Shem and Japheth took a garment, laid it on both their shoulders, and went backward and covered the nakedness of their father. Their faces were turned away, and they did not see their father's nakedness" (Gen. 9:23).

When Canaan was cursed, Shem and Japheth were blessed. "Blessed be the Lord, the God of Shem" (Gen. 9:26). How was Shem blessed? "May God enlarge Japheth, and may he dwell in the tents of Shem; and may Canaan be his servant" (Gen. 9:27).

As a result of Shem's blessing, he was identified with the worship of Jehovah, and has been recognized as a group of people with dominant spiritual motives. Ultimately, the woman's seed, i.e., the Messiah, came from the family of Shem, through Abraham, and the Jews. Jesus ultimately came from the line of Shem.

God also promised to bless Japheth. The Japhetic peoples are Greeks, Romans, Arians, Europeans, and they have been those who have supplied scientific discovery, philosophers, and been the driving force behind western civilization.

Why curse Canaan? Ham was the youngest son of Noah, and Canaan was the youngest son of Ham (Gen. 10:6). Just as people say that the youngest child of the family is the spoiled one, so Ham and Canaan were the youngest in the family i.e., perhaps they received the less amount of attention, discipline, and direction.

A divine curse. When Noah cursed Canaan, this was not just an "angry" grandfather who was punishing his grandson. No! Only God knows the future, so only God knew what the Canaanites would be like long after Noah and his sons were dead. So, God cursed Canaan through Noah, because of what would happen to Canaan and his sons, i.e., the Canaanites. God spoke a curse through Noah on Canaan for what he did to his grandfather Noah, predicting that his descendants would do the same thing in the future, hence would be judged by God.

God revealed a weakness in both Ham and Canaan because their sexual weakness would be perpetuated in the Canaanites who occupied the Promised Land. When Noah said, "Cursed be Canaan; A servant of servants He shall be to his brethren" (Gen. 9:25), God was applying the principle that He said elsewhere, i.e., that the third and fourth generation would be punished for the sins of their forefathers, because they too will continue in that sin. "For I, the LORD your God, am a jealous God, visiting the iniquity of the fathers upon the children to the third and fourth generations of those who hate Me" (Exod. 20:5). Did you see that phrase, "hate Me?" Implied in the sin of Canaan, is a rejection of God, perhaps even hatred of God. This young boy who lived one generation from the flood, was not grateful for the Lord's deliverance through the flood. Rather than showing respect for a grandfather who was used of God, young Canaan "thumbed his nose" at both Noah and the God of Noah.

When was Canaan's curse carried out? Some Christians, primarily those from the segregated part of the United States, teach that the curse is on the black man who originally came from Africa happened when some became slaves to the white man. This obviously is an attempt to justify slavery and segregation. But that view is wrong for more than one reason. First, because the curse was on Canaan, not on Ham. It was Ham who went to Africa, Canaan went to the land named after him, i.e., Canaan. Second, the curse was on Canaan and the Canaanites who lived in the Promised Land. That curse was carried out when God's people—Hebrews, not whites—were led by Joshua to conquer the Promised Land and drive out the Canaanites.

Throughout the early books of Scripture, the Canaanites are described as a lustful people. At one place God described them with an unusual phrase, "uncovered their nakedness" (Lev. 18:3ff), perhaps a description that has its roots in the original reason why God used Israel to drive the Canaanites from Canaan.

WHAT GRANDPARENTS SHOULD KNOW ABOUT SIN

You never get too old to sin. Some people think that the older they get, the godlier they become. They don't usually see older people involved in sexual sins, stealing, or the other outward physical sins. So, they equate the sedate nature of the older people with godliness. But, just being quiet and meek does not make a person godly. To be godly, one must get close to God. To be spiritual one must be filled with the Holy Spirit (Eph. 5:18).

Remember as a young man Solomon served the Lord and wrote the beautiful Song of Solomon. It was the middle-aged Solomon who pursued women, and the bitter old Solomon who wrote the book of Ecclesiastes where he said, "Vanity of vanities, all is vanity" (Eccl. 1:2).

You can fall at your greatest strength. Often in the Bible when God's people fell into sin, they didn't usually fall at their weakness, rather they usually fell at their strength. Abraham was a man of great faith, but in weakness he lied about his wife. God called Moses the meekest man on the face of the earth, yet in pride he smote the rock. Elijah was a bold prophet, yet one word from Jezebel set him running away. Solomon was the wisest man on the face of the earth, yet he "chased skirts." And Peter was also the bold disciple, but he denied the Lord with a curse when a little maid challenged him. That means older people can fall at their strength, not weakness. Paul warns us, "Therefore let him who thinks he stands take heed lest he fall" (1 Cor. 10:12).

Your fall can hurt your family. You never sin alone, your sin like a rock thrown into a pond, creates endless ripples that ultimately will reach the shore. Every sin you commit will have an influence on your children, and grandchildren. Noah's sins certainly condemned his grandson Canaan.

Your sin can come after God has greatly used you. Some of God's greatest leaders had a relapse after they were used greatly of God. On Mount Carmel, Elijah confronted the prophets of Baal, prayed fire out of Heaven and later prayed rain out of Heaven (it had not rained for three and half years) (Jas. 5:17-18). Yet Elijah ran away from Jezebel, became depressed, and questioned God. Peter was the leader of the twelve disciples but denied the Lord. David drove the enemies out of the Promised Land, and became king over all twelve tribes of Israel; but after great victories, committed adultery with Bathsheba, and was responsible for the murder of Uriah. We read godly King Azziah fortified Israel, yet at the end of his reign became arrogant. He went into the house of God, invaded the office of the priest and tried to sacrifice to God. God immediately struck him with leprosy, and he had to abdicate his throne. It is possible to be greatly used of God, then lose your effectiveness in your last days.

Just because you've done much for God in the past, doesn't mean He will overlook sin in your old age. There is no such thing as supererogation whereby you can build up good works in Heaven to compensate for future sins. Every sin stands for itself, just like every good work will have its own reward. A truthful God cannot overlook your sin, just like He will not deny reward for what you do good.

A careless root of sin in a grandfather can have disastrous results in grandchildren. Sometimes older people become careless in their walk for God. Maybe they've sinned several times, and each time God has forgiven and restored them. This can produce a cavalier approach to iniquity. Therefore, aged people who know much, think they know enough to get away with sin. But it's not true; look again at the case of Noah's disastrous results on Canaan.

Drunkenness is not a private sin, nor is it something God overlooks. Some people think that they harm only themselves when they get drunk. A drunk doesn't say, "Leave me alone," claiming "I'm not hurting anyone." But that's not true. A drunk doesn't have a positive influence on others. A drunk is not a role model of God's grace. A drunk is not influencing children and grandchildren into righteousness. A drunk is not "filled with the spirit" but they are "filled with wine." Paul has told us, "And do not be drunk with wine, in which is dissipation; but be filled with the Spirit" (Eph. 5:18).

The child of God must be modest because the body is the Temple of the Holy Spirit. Obviously almost everyone has looked at naked little babies, because almost everyone has changed diapers. Why is that we begin to think that nakedness is nothing? Is that why after we get older, we take a cavalier approach to nakedness?

Honestly, the body is a beautiful thing, and in certain works of art, people admire the beauty and artistic form of a human body. But nakedness...and lust...and evil desires are tied to the wrong display of the body, and the wrong viewing of nakedness. Modesty of the body has always been a Christian virtue. The body is the temple of the Holy Spirit (1 Cor. 6:18-20). It is a sanctuary because God lives in us; therefore, we must be careful to always glorify God with the body.

- Applies to all ages
- Applies to sexual exposure
- Applies to sexual viewing, i.e., lust

Repressed lust and sexual fantasies usually surface when given the opportunity. Apparently, Canaan had some internally negative attitudes toward Noah and the Lord God. When given the opportunity to mock

God's man—Noah—Canaan was quick to seize the opportunity. What Canaan said to his father Ham reflected the attitude of his heart.

Sometimes children can be raised in a Christian home, and repress their sexual or rebellious attitudes. But when given an opportunity, "What's in the well comes up in the bucket." When people don't discipline themselves, sin usually finds a way to express itself in looks, attitudes, and actions.

WHAT GRANDCHILDREN NEED TO KNOW

God provides victory. There is an internal battle between good and evil, and God has provided that every child can overcome temptation. When you daily pray the Lord's Prayer, you ask, "Lead us not into temptation" (Matt. 6:10). As you make that request, claim victory because. "No temptation has overtaken you except such as is common to man; but God is faithful, who will not allow you to be tempted beyond what you are able, but with the temptation will also make the way of escape, that you may be able to bear it" (1 Cor. 10:13).

God lives in your body. In this dispensation, God is not living in a tabernacle in the wilderness, nor does He live in a sanctuary like Solomon's Temple in Jerusalem. Rather, God seeks a sanctuary, i.e., the sanctuary of your body. As Paul said, ". . . Christ lives in me" (Gal. 2:20). But that's not just living in your mind, Christ actually lives in your body. Notice what Paul says, "Flee sexual immorality. Every sin that a man does is outside the body, but he who commits sexual immorality sins against his own body. Or do you not know that your body is the temple of the Holy Spirit who is in you, whom you have from God, and you are not your own?" (1 Cor. 6:18-19).

What did Noah do? He filled his body with alcohol, rather than filling his life with God. What was Ham's reaction? Surely, he didn't take a godly approach to the sin of his grandfather. And what was Canaan's reaction? He went farther than any other reaction, his sin was greatest of all. If Ham and Canaan had sought the glory of God and the restoration of his grandfather, the curse of Canaan would have never happened.

The old age sin will disqualify you. What is old age sin? It's running the race well, but giving up when you're almost to the finish line. It's living for God all of your life, but denying God when you reach retirement. It's treating your "golden years" as an opportunity to give up Sunday school teaching, church attendance, and the opportunity to influence your grandchildren.

Paul challenged us to run a race. "Do you not know that those who run in a race all run, but one receives the prize? Run in such a way that you may obtain it" (1 Cor. 9:24). What was that prize that you would obtain? Paul says that we must discipline ourselves as a runner, so we can make it to the finish line. "But I discipline my body and bring it into subjection, lest, when I have preached to others, I myself should become disqualified" (1 Cor. 9:27).

Chapter Six

LOIS: GRANDMOTHER OF TIMOTHY

SPEAKING THE WORDS OF SCRIPTURE INTO A GRANDSON

Grandmother – Lois

Mother – Eunice

Grandson – Timothy

"Then he (Paul) came to Derbe and Lystra. And behold, a certain disciple was there, named Timothy, the son of a certain Jewish woman who believed, but his father was Greek. He was well spoken of by the brethren who were at Lystra and Iconium. Paul wanted to have him go on with him. And he took him and circumcised him because of the Jews who were in that region, for they all knew that his father was Greek" (Acts 16:1-3).

"When I call to remembrance the genuine faith that is in you, which dwelt first in your grandmother Lois and your mother Eunice, and I am persuaded is in you also" (2 Timothy 1:5).

"But you must continue in the things which you have learned and been assured of, knowing from whom you have learned them, and that from childhood you have known the Holy Scriptures, which are able to make you wise for salvation through faith which is in Christ Jesus" (2 Timothy 3:14, 15).

MY name is Lois, and I was born in Lystra, a small town in the mountains. It was an out-of-the-way place; not many people came to visit, so we didn't know a lot about what was happening in the world. There was not much culture or civilization in Lystra.

I was born of Jewish parents, but there were only a few Jewish families in Lystra. So, when it came to getting married, there were no Jewish boys available. A visiting rabbi said, "Better marry a Gentile man and drag him into Heaven, than not marry at all." So I married a Gentile man. But my husband said, that if we have a boy, he could not be circumcised or wear the Jewish Judenhut and the special kippah or prayer hat. But we had a beautiful black-headed girl and I gave her a Greek name Eunice, meaning "commended well."

When it came time for Eunice to marry, she faced the same problems, the same limitations as I because there were no Jewish boys available, so she married a Greek. He told my daughter the same thing my husband told me, that if they were to have a son, he could not be circumcised or raised as a Jew, or be dressed as a Jew.

Both Eunice and I knew the baby would be a boy, and before he was born we dedicated him to God. We knew the stories of great Jewish heroes and we wanted him to be a great man of God. We knew the stories of Jewish boys who grew up outside the Holy Land—Moses...

Daniel...Nehemiah...Ezra...and wanted our boy to be greatly used of God.

That little boy didn't stand a chance with both of us. When I was teaching, little Timothy learned the Law, the prophecies, and the great principles of God's Word. When Eunice was teaching him, he learned the psalms, to pray, and to passionately love God.

When he could barely run through the house, I taught him how to begin writing. I showed him how to cut the end off a feather for a pen. I showed him how to mix crushed charcoal and olive oil to make ink. We even made paper, crushing the papyrus reed into flat sheets. We dried the wet paper in the sun. Then I showed him to hold the feather between his forefinger and thumb and squeeze the barrel of the feather so the ink came out. He first wrote an *alaph*, the first letter of the alphabet. Then a *beth*, and next a *gimel*. For me, little Timothy copied the Law. For Eunice, little Timothy copied the Psalms and Proverbs.

One day Paul showed up in Lystra and gathered all the Jewish people together. There were not enough Jews in our town to have a synagogue, so we gathered in a large home. When Paul taught the Scriptures, I then believed that Jesus was the Messiah. I believed that Jesus was the Son of God. My daughter Eunice believed and so did Timothy. We believed because Paul showed us in the Scriptures that Messiah was to suffer, be killed, and rise again the third day.

Shortly after Paul arrived in town, outsiders showed up to argue with him. They attacked him and stoned him, dragging him outside town. Some of our people said he was badly hurt. Others said he was killed. I don't know what happened, but God did a miracle. He got up from the road, and walked back into town. We were all amazed...we rejoiced...we praised God.

That was two years ago, but now Paul is back in Lystra. He's heading off into the wilderness where it will be dangerous; he wants Timothy to go with him. That's not my decision, nor is it Eunice's decision. That's Timothy's decision. If Timothy goes along to help Paul, it'll be a dangerous trip. Timothy could even be stoned, like Paul was here in Lystra.

I hate to think about the death of a grandson, but I'm willing to give him up to the Lord Jesus Christ. Since Jesus suffered for us, what more could we do than give Him our all. And if Timothy gives his entire life to the Lord Jesus Christ, what better fulfillment can Eunice or I have than to realize that we taught a young man the Word of God, and now he'll use his life for the glory of God.

Be a grandparent who overcomes insurmountable odds, and limited resources, and difficult circumstances, to influence your grandchildren to win battles, do exploits and achieve greatness for God.

GRANDMOTHER SPEAKS INTO YOUNG LIFE

Lessons to Take Away

When grandparents have limited resources and face barriers, they can motivate their grandchildren to greatness by speaking the Word of God into their lives.

Lois was influential in the life of her grandson, even though everything seemed to be against her. She had married outside the Hebrew religion, there was not a Hebrew synagogue to help teach her daughter and grandson, and she was isolated in a mountain town, cut off from civilization and cultural advantages.

Lois spoke the words of Scripture into Timothy so that he became an indispensable helper to the apostle Paul and the primary church leaders after the apostles had all died. The words Lois and Eunice spoke into Timothy became the foundation that guided Timothy's influential life.

If a grandmother speaks negative words, or words of discouragement into a grandchild, the young life will probably focus on what it can't do. If a grandmother speaks words of anger and bitterness into a child, the young person will probably be driven by temper or an irrational spirit. When a grandmother speaks words of greatness into a young child, that growing life will probably aspire to overcome difficulties.

Grandmother Lois married a Gentile. The Bible describes two women who were influential in the life of Timothy. The first woman was Lois who was married to a Gentile, just as her daughter Eunice also married a Greek. "A certain disciple was there, named Timothy, the son of a certain Jewish woman (Eunice) who believed, but his father was Greek" (Acts 16:1). This verse suggests the influence of a mother on a daughter. As the mother Lois had lived, so grew the daughter, Eunice. They both married Greeks. Maybe there were no eligible Jewish young men. Some think Lois might have rebelled against her Jewish upbringing to marry a Gentile in her desire to throw off her cultural shackles. If this is true, somewhere along the line Lois came back to her roots. Lois then taught her daughter Eunice Hebrew godliness, but also taught her grandson Timothy the Scriptures. However, this doesn't seem to be the case. Paul describes the "unfeigned faith" of Lois. She had a simple faith that was genuine and unhypocritical. Lois probably married a Gentile because there were no other options.

Life in the mountain town of Lystra. When Paul went into a new town, he began preaching in the Jewish synagogue, but no synagogue is mentioned in Lystra. This is probably because there were not enough Jews to form a synagogue (the Jewish rabbis insisted that it took twelve Jewish families to build a synagogue).

Lystra was off the beaten path up in the mountains, and Roman historians indicate that there were very few Roman citizens that lived there. As a result, there was very little cultural advantages or Roman civilization. Also, Derbe and Lystra were not on the main highways, hence, travelers didn't pass through Lystra; only people who had business in Lystra visited there. As result, the people of Lystra heard and experienced very little about the outside world.

Grandma Lois expected a son but got a daughter. Every Jewish woman expected her first child to be a son that she would dedicate as a rabbi. The next sons in the family would either be doctors, lawyers, teachers, or some other honorable profession. But Lois didn't have a son; she had a daughter Eunice, whose name means *commended*. God commended the home of Lois and her husband with a little baby girl.

Like mother like daughter. Just as Lois had married a Gentile husband and probably agreed to raise her sons in Gentile tradition, her daughter Eunice had the same marriage bond and made the same type of agreement. When Timothy was born to Eunice, he was not circumcised. Later when Timothy began following Paul, the apostle "wanted to have him (Timothy) go on with him. And he took him and circumcised him because of the Jews who were in that region, for they all knew that his father was Greek" (Acts 16:3).

Grandma Lois had genuine faith. While some think she compromised in marrying a Gentile, that is probably not the case. Paul commends her saying, "When I call to remembrance the unfeigned faith that is in thee, which dwelt first in thy grandmother Lois" (2 Tim. 1:5, KJV). The word *unfeigned* means genuine, and comes from the actors in a theater who played a role. When an actor would play a role on stage, he would wear a mask. But Lois had true faith, she was not playing a Christian role and she didn't wear a mask. Her faith was genuine.

Lois and Eunice poured their faith into Timothy. As they influenced Timothy, they taught the young child the Jewish Scriptures, making sure that he not only knew them in his head, but also accepted them in his heart. Paul told Timothy, "Continue in the things which you have learned and been assured of, knowing from whom you have learned them" (2 Tim. 3:14). The word "whom" is plural, suggesting Timothy was taught by both Lois and Eunice.

If one woman was strong in the devotional life, i.e., the Psalms, pouring spirituality into Timothy, the other woman was strong in the law or God's standards, pouring character into his life. Together the two women taught Timothy all of the Scriptures, and made him a strong disciple.

The word "knowing" is *oida*, which means Timothy didn't have just head knowledge, but innate knowledge. The women molded inner character into the life of young Timothy. He was obedient, not just when his mother was watching; he was obedient when no one was watching.

Character is always doing the right thing in the right way.

When Paul told Timothy to continue in the things that you have been assured, he was suggesting that the two women laid the foundation for Timothy's conversion. How Timothy began his Christian life, is the way he continued serving the Lord.

Lois and Eunice began teaching young Timothy very early. Paul notes that, "from childhood you have known the Holy Scriptures, which are able to make you wise" (2 Tim. 3:15). The word "childhood" is *brethos*, which means embryo or a newborn baby. Long before Timothy could talk, the women began teaching him the Scriptures. Probably the women sang the psalms of Israel to him as they rocked or cuddled him in their arms. When they taught him to count the numbers, they probably repeated the Ten Commandments. When they taught him his "ABCs," they probably identified with the great heroes of the Bible, i.e., A is for Abraham the father of faith, B is for Bathsheba the mother of Solomon, etc.

When Paul says that Timothy knew "the Holy Scriptures," he uses the Greek word *graphe*, which are the writings. This suggests first, a child would learn the Scriptures while copying the Scriptures. This is the way scribes learned the Bible. Timothy probably copied great portions of the Scriptures for his own personal possession. But second, the word *writings* is plural, suggesting that he didn't just learn the Scripture as an overall unit, but he learned each of the many parts of Scripture, giving attention to each book in the Old Testament. The women did their job well.

Lois and Eunice had a purpose in teaching young Timothy the Scriptures. They were to "make him wise unto salvation." Even a small preposition gives us insight into the way Timothy's grandmother and mother influenced him. The preposition *"eis"* suggests the women were always moving Timothy "into" salvation. They wanted him to be a good Jew in his heart, even though he didn't bear on his body the marks of circumcision.

Lois and Eunice prepared the spiritual foundation for Timothy's conversion. Eventually when Paul came to Lystra, Timothy believed in Jesus Christ. Why? Paul says, "When I call to remembrance the genuine faith that is in you, which dwelt first in your grandmother Lois and your mother Eunice, and I am persuaded is in you also" (2 Tim. 1:5). The pure, unfeigned faith of both Lois and Eunice was poured into the life of young Timothy, and he too had unfeigned faith. The soft feminine hands that caressed the baby's brow also pointed the direction in which the child eventually walked.

PAUL BUILT ON THE INFLUENCE OF LOIS AND EUNICE

Some godly children are influenced by a godly father, and when that happens; God is glorified. In other occasions a godly child is influenced by a mother or a grandmother; and again, God is magnified.

Lois and Eunice believed that Jesus was the Messiah during Paul's first trip to Lystra. When Paul first came to Lystra (Acts 14:6-23), he gathered the few Jews together and announced to them that Jesus Christ was the Messiah, that He died and rose again to give them new life. It was then that Lois and Eunice became believers, probably Timothy also. How do we know? When Paul arrived in Lystra on his second missionary journey, it was noted that Eunice was already a believer. "Then he (Paul) came to Derbe and Lystra. And behold, a certain disciple was there, named Timothy, the son of a certain Jewish woman who believed, but his father was Greek (Acts 16:1). The word *believed* is in the past tense, suggesting that Eunice believed in Jesus the first time Paul came to her city. Since the two women are joined in ministry Second Timothy 1:5 suggests that Lois also believed in Jesus that first time Paul came to Lystra.

Timothy believed in Christ under Paul's ministry. Probably Timothy was saved under the Old Testament dispensation. He and the women were good believing Jews who followed the teachings of the Scripture. And in the Old Testament dispensation, if they had died before hearing about Jesus Christ, they would have gone to Heaven. How do we know this is true? Because when the message of Jesus was preached to them, they believed.

There's another reason to believe Timothy believed in Christ when Paul came to Lystra the first time. Twice, Paul calls him a son, i.e., spiritual son, "To Timothy, a true son in the faith" (1 Tim. 1:2) and "To Timothy, my beloved son" (2 Tim. 1:2). This is a relationship of love and esteem.

Timothy believed in spite of persecution. When Paul finally arrived at Lystra, he began preaching and not much happened. Then Paul healed a man at the city gate who was crippled from birth. This astounding miracle shocked the people of Lystra. They thought the gods had come down to them, i.e., Jupiter and Mercury. The people wanted to sacrifice an ox to Paul and Barnabas, but Paul rejected their offer and turned their attention to the God of Creation. He exhorted the people that "you should turn from these useless things to the living God, who made the heaven, the earth, the sea, and all things that are in them" (Acts 14:15). Young Timothy must have been impressed when he saw his "substitute father-figure" turn down crowd adoration and point people to the Living God.

But that's not the end of the story. Jews who hated Paul's message followed him from Antioch and Iconium, stirred up the town's people so that they stoned Paul. Notice who did the stoning. "The Jews...stoned Paul and dragged him out of the city, supposing him to be dead" (Acts 14:19). Timothy was probably an eyewitness to this execution.

Some believed that Paul was badly hurt but was able to get up and leave town the following day. They only "supposed" he was dead. Others believe Paul actually died. When he got up, it was God's raising him from the dead. This is probably the case, and later Paul suggests that during this occasion, he actually died and went to Heaven, "I know a man in Christ who fourteen years ago...such a one was caught up to the third heaven. And I know such a man—whether in the body or out of the body I do not know, God knows; how he was caught up into Paradise and heard inexpressible words, which it is not lawful for a man to utter" (2 Cor. 12:1-4). Because of what Paul saw and experienced in Heaven, he was given a "thorn in his flesh" for the rest of his life to remind him of his frailty and humanity.

Whether Paul was killed or not, Timothy witnessed the vicious persecution. But the attacks on Paul did not dampen Timothy's faith, nor did it turn away his decision to follow Jesus Christ. If anything, it probably put resolve in the young man's heart to be willing to suffer persecution also for God.

Later, Paul writes to remind Timothy of what happened in Lystra, "But you have carefully followed my doctrine, manner of life...persecutions, afflictions, which happened to me at Antioch, at Iconium, at Lystra" (2 Tim. 3:10-11).

Timothy was recommended by church leaders at Lystra. Not only was the young child Timothy well trained by Lois and Eunice, the people in the community respected young Timothy. When Paul came through the city on his second missionary journey, he invited Timothy to go with him to help him in ministry. The elders in the church at Lystra supported that decision. They not only thought it was a good idea, they were willing to go on record by ordaining young Timothy into ministry. Paul notes this event when he writes, "Do not neglect the gift that is in you, which was given to you by prophecy with the laying on of the hands of the eldership" (1 Tim. 4:14).

Timothy was ordained by Paul. After the leading elders in Lystra recommended Timothy for ministry, then Paul also laid hands on Timothy, setting him apart for ministry. Paul exhorted Timothy to keep on "stirring up the gift of God which is in you through the laying on of my hands" (2 Tim. 1:6). The words "stirring up" is in the continuous action, meaning Timothy was the type of a man who had to constantly challenge himself to use spiritual gifts for the ministry of God.

LESSONS TO TAKE AWAY

When a grandmother has many limitations, she can still be a great influence for God through her children and grandchildren. In the natural realm there was not much that Lois and Eunice could do for the kingdom of God. But through young Timothy, their influence reached throughout the Mediterranean world. Their influence transcended time. When Paul needed help in his travels to the different churches, Lois and Eunice were there in the life of Timothy. When Paul was in prison in Rome, Lois and Eunice came to his assistance through Timothy. When Paul needed a preacher in the great city of Ephesus, Lois and Eunice answered the call through the ministry of Timothy.

Children do not become godly automatically; it takes initiative, focus, and commitment. Lois and Eunice made Timothy the focus of their life, so he received their love and attention.

John Wesley has given us good direction in how to teach young children. Stan Toler has shared with me the four principles John Wesley used to teach children.

Wesley's Principles of Teaching Children

1. Early instruction.
2. Plain instruction.
3. Frequent instruction.
4. Patient instruction.

A grandmother's home can have great godly influence, even when a church is not available to help. Lois did not have the advantage of a full synagogue to assist in training Eunice or young Timothy. A synagogue is a place of teaching, where a rabbi would have taught the children the Hebrew language, the Law, as well as the basic necessities of life. Young Timothy probably did not have access to such a teacher or a rabbi. But what he didn't have in a male teacher, Lois and Eunice probably made up with "home schooling." As a matter of fact, they might be the prototypes of the modern home school movement. If so, perhaps young children will come from modern day home schools to equal the influence of Timothy.

Every grandmother needs the help of a godly male role model to influence her grandsons.

As great as the influence of Lois and Eunice were on young Timothy, Paul made all the difference in the world when he came on the scene. The apostle supplied the male role model. The preaching, ministry, and example of Paul impacted young Timothy.

And why did Paul choose Lystra when there were so many cities in Asia Minor? He could have been led there by the sovereignty of God, but it might have been an answer to the prayers of Lois and Eunice who wanted young Timothy to be a great influence for God. And through the influence of Paul, Timothy became all that his grandmother and mother wanted him to become.

Giving great attention to small details in children's education will influence their entire life. When Paul describes Timothy, knowing the "holy" writings, he implies that Timothy had copied the Scriptures, memorized the Scriptures, but more than that, believed the Scriptures and lived by the Scriptures. Grandma Lois and his mother Eunice had done their job well. When a grandmother can't be all she wants to be in life, at least she can be faithful in what God has given her to do. We don't know the dreams of Grandmother Lois, but we do know that she was faithful in training her young grandson, young Timothy. Because of her "unfeigned faith," she poured that faith into Timothy, and he was used in the foundation of missionary work throughout the Mediterranean world.

Chapter Seven

PAUL: A SPIRITUAL GRANDFATHER

A DISCIPLE-MAKING GRANDPARENT

Spiritual Grandfather – Paul

Son in ministry – Timothy

Third Generation – Faithful men

Fourth Generation – Others

"And the things that you have heard from me among many witnesses, commit these to faithful men who will be able to teach others also" (2 Timothy 2:2).

MY name is Timothy. I was born and grew up in a little out-of-the-way mountain village called Lystra. My father was a Gentile who did not follow the God of the Old Testament, but he allowed my grandmother Lois and my mother Eunice—both godly Jewish women—to teach me the Word of God and made sure that I obeyed the God of the Old Testament. Like all good Jewish boys, I was looking for the Messiah. When the apostle Paul came to Lystra, preaching the Lord Jesus Christ, I believed Jesus was the Messiah, and Jesus became my Savior. I remember the first time Paul took me aside, encouraging me to serve the Lord. He took time to answer all my questions. Over the years Paul became my substitute father, and my role model; I decided to be like Paul when I became a man.

When Paul came through our village on his second missionary journey, he asked me to travel with the team. At first, I took care of the luggage, and the tickets, and the meals, and the lodging. Paul was run out of Thessalonica by a mob of hateful Jews; he left me there to preach. I had seen Paul stoned by another mob and I knew it could happen to me, but I was willing to die for the Lord.

On two or three other occasions, Paul sent me to preach and build up the young churches. Finally, I became pastor of Ephesus, that great church where Paul had preached. Paul not only taught me the Word of God, but he gave me responsibilities to serve the Lord, so I'd grow stronger in character for the Lord Jesus Christ.

My life won't be complete until I influence another young man, like Paul influenced me. I'll have to teach another young man doctrine and give him other responsibilities so he can grow in spiritual character, just as I've grown. And then, that young disciple that I train will have to influence still another young disciple. What Paul poured into me, will have to be poured into other young leaders until the Great Commission is completed, and the world is won to Jesus Christ.

WHAT GRANDPARENTS DO THAT PARENTS DON'T DO

Grandparents can deal in positive gentleness, while parents must correct because of negative consequences. The very nature of being a parent means they must deal with the things children do wrong. Parents must deal both negatively to correct, and positively to build them up. Paul gave both views when he said, "Father, provoke not your children to wrath (negative), but bring them up in the nurture and admonition (positive) of the Lord" (Eph. 6:4). Both negative and positive influences are needed to bring up a child with a balanced view of life. In a negative sense, the Book of Proverbs exhorts, "Correct thy son, and he shall give thee rest" (Prov. 29:17, KJV). And in a positive sense, the Book of Proverbs said, "Now therefore, listen to me, my children, for blessed are those who keep my ways" (Prov. 8:32).

Good grandparents don't have to deal with a child's disobedience and troubles, unless it directly involves the grandparents. When grandchildren walk through the door of their grandparents' home, a new leaf is turned, and a clear page appears. All the problems a child had at home are forgotten when grandmother cooks for them, or grandpa begins telling stories. Grandparents treat the child with more maturity—forgetting failures—and the child will respond to the positive assessment of their grandparents. Because grandparents think the child is much more grown up than they are—and treat them that way—the child responds by acting grown up.

Grandparents point out your future greatness, while parents must deal with your present shortcomings. The difference here is in focus, grandparents usually have a long-range focus, because they see the big picture of life. Grandparents are exhorted, "A good man leaves an inheritance to his children's children" (Prov. 13:22). Because of grandparents' long look, the Psalmist promises, "Yes, may you see your children's children" (Ps. 128:6). But parents have to deal with their children's disobedience. "Foolishness is bound in the heart of a child; but the rod of correction should drive it far from him" (Prov. 22:15) Also, parents are exhorted to "withhold not correction of the child" (Prov. 23:13). And what about the permissive parent? "But a child left to himself brings shame to his mother" (Prov. 29:15).

Grandparents can build individual imitative, while parents must teach responsibility and accountability. Basically, both parents are necessary. Grandparents and parents deal in both negative and positive areas, i.e., both deal with the child's rebellion (negative) and both deal with the child's ambition (positive). However, for the most part grandparents can build up a child's initiative because they can focus on the grandchild's assertiveness and inquisitiveness. But parents must focus on accountability, "Children, obey your parents in all things, for this is well pleasing to the Lord" (Col. 3:20). Paul knew when children were obedient to parents, they would be obedient to all types of authority (political, business, school, church, etc). But at the same time, Paul expressed moderation to the Colossians, "Fathers, do not provoke your children, lest they become discouraged" (Col. 3:21).

Grandparents have learned what is eternally important and what immediately can be overlooked. The Bible speaks continually of a person's "children's children" meaning that grandchildren are our inheritance. Grandparents should rejoice in them, plan for them, leave money to them, and show love to them.

WHAT IS A DISCIPLE-MAKING GRANDPARENT?

A disciple-making grandparent must be a reproducer of reproducers. A parent can rejoice in a child, as the Bible has said, "Behold, children are a heritage from the LORD" (Ps. 127:3). "Happy is the man who has his quiver full of them (children)" (Ps. 127:5). But not everyone who has children goes the second mile to correctly rear that child. That's because anyone who has sex can potentially give birth, but it takes something more than sex to be a parent. Sadly, many who have sex outside of marriage are thinking of their own satisfaction. They're not thinking long-range, i.e., they forget that a child can be born out of sexual intercourse. When children are born, there is a responsibility for training and influencing them

on this earth, but what about their children, and their children's children? Every child that is born has the potential of producing children like themselves, and grandchildren like themselves. That's why God instituted marriage. The home is a classroom; it's a place where a child is taught principles how to live. And what parents can't teach, God has given grandparents to energize, motivate, and guide the child to fulfill his/her destiny.

Obviously, most will reproduce themselves physically. But what about reproducing ourselves spiritually, emotionally, socially, and don't forget basic needs, i.e., food, clothing and shelter? Every parent must reproduce themselves in their children. And they have done a good job when their children reproduce themselves in every way in their grandchildren.

The Bible teaches that parents are to pour their life into children, so that children may walk on this earth as parents have walked. The Book of Deuteronomy instructs, "These words which I command you today shall be in your heart. You shall teach them diligently to your children, and shall talk of them when you sit in your house, when you walk by the way, when you lie down, and when you rise up" (Deut. 6:6-7). This means child-rearing is an all-time responsibility of teaching children to live godly as parents have lived before God.

But what about grandparents? If grandparents pour their life into their children, then their children will live as they live. That's the goal, reproducing grandparents whose children and children's children live as their grandparents. They must love God as the grandparents love God, and serve God as the grandparents served God.

Some parents may try to "beat" a child into submission (obviously, that's not the way to do it), and the child may live outwardly a Christian life, but because they have been "beaten" into submission, the child has not inwardly taken on the values and attitudes of their parent. As soon as the child gets away from their parents, they become prodigals. The child rejects all that the parent "beat" into them. However, the goal is for grandchildren to live the way his parents and grandparents taught him, "Children's children are the crown of old men, and the glory of children is their father" (Prov. 17:6).

Disciple-making grandparents will outlive their lessons. The way you live before your children and grandchildren will stretch into the future beyond your life. So, how you treat your children is the way they will treat their children. Hence, the way you treat our children will make you a good grandparent. To become a godly reproducer of godly grandchildren you must produce godliness into your children.

Children are mimickers, they follow examples, and not necessarily what is told them. That means the lessons of childhood are more "caught," than "taught." You can tell your children to love other people and to share their toys, but if they see and feel your selfish attitudes, they won't become a "giving person."

Paul told Timothy; four generations is the "acid test" of child-rearing credibility. Paul (the first generation) poured his life into Timothy (the second generation) who poured his life into faithful men (the third generation); they did the same to others (fourth generation). That means you must pour your life into your children; they in turn must pour that life into your grandchildren. But your grandchildren are not really *reproducers of reproducers* until your great grandchildren live the same way you live. Hence, it takes four generations before you become a *reproducer of reproducers.*

Paul	You
Timothy	Your children
Faithful man	Your grandchildren
Others	Your great grandchildren

Reproducing grandparents pour their souls into grandchildren. Paul did not just share the Gospel with those he won to Christ. Notice, he poured his total life into new converts, "We were gentle among you, just as a nursing mother cherishes her own children. So, affectionately longing for you, we were well pleased to impart to you not only the gospel of God, but also our own lives, because you had become dear to us" (1 Thess. 2:7-8, author's translation). What does a nursing mother do for her child? She loves...she protects...she provides...she encourages...she gives life-giving food. That's what a reproducing grandparent must do for both children and grandchildren.

Disciple-making grandparents become necessary to grandchildren. When you begin to build a foundation into your children or grandchildren, they depend on you for strength and guidance. Just as a foundation gives direction and determines the size of the building, so reproducing grandparents determine the future of their children and grandchildren. Children do not always understand all that they need to do, nor do they understand how they are to live. They depend upon parents and grandparents for continued direction in their life. Therefore, grandparents have a disciple-making role in their life.

Disciple-making is not something you do once, and you're finished. Disciple-making is not a one-time event; rather, disciple-making is a continuous lifetime activity. You become a disciple-maker in informal times as you talk with them while riding in the car, by example as you read the Scriptures, by counsel as you coach them how to repair something, or as you direct them through complicated relationships with others.

Disciple-making grandparents have not finished until their grandchildren pour into others, what you have poured into them. The acid test of a disciple-maker is their disciples. Proverbs said, "The just man walks in his integrity; his children are blessed after him" (Prov. 20:7). And what does that mean?

"Children's children are the crown of old men" (Prov. 17:6). The disciple-maker who has good children is described as having fruitful children, i.e., "Your children like olive plants all around your table" (Ps. 128:3). The grandparents who follow the Lord are blessed of Him, "Yes, may you see your children's children" (Ps. 128:6).

WHAT DOES A DISCIPLE LOOK LIKE?

A disciple of Jesus Christ doesn't look anything like the typical American church member. There are a lot of Christians who are just typical American church members, and maybe many of them will go to Heaven; but their lives do not compare with those who followed Jesus in the First Century.

Too many American church members do not attend church on a regular basis as a statement of their devotion to the Lord. They attend when it's convenient or they give God a little money, but they have never approached the level of sacrificial giving. They seldom dig into the Scriptures, nor are they regular prayer intercessors. The typical American church member knows nothing of soul winning, nor investing their lives in ministry. Therefore, if you are a grandparent who wants to disciple your grandchildren, you need to know what a disciple looks like. Before you can become a disciple-maker for your children or grandchildren, you must first become a follower of Jesus Christ.

A disciple makes a radical decision for salvation. A disciple is not just someone who makes a superficial decision to believe in God, they make a *radical decision* that changes their entire life. Salvation is more than head belief that God exists, and it is more than an emotional stirring of the heart, and it is more than saying "yes" with one's will. It takes a total life-commitment to Jesus Christ. Salvation involves all three: intellect, emotion, and will; as these three elements

of your personality respond positively to the Word of God, but discipleship involves your physical life, your family life, your business life...everything! Through the Bible we are saved, "So then faith comes by hearing, and hearing by the word of God" (Rom. 10:17). Through the Word of God, we are born again and receive a new nature, "Of His own will He brought us forth by the word of truth" (James 1:18). Those who respond to His invitation to follow Jesus Christ are actually obeying His words, because as God, Jesus spoke the Word of God, "If anyone desires to come after Me, let him deny himself, and take up his cross daily, and follow Me" (Luke 9:23).

A disciple dedicates himself to be like Jesus. Not only must we make a decision to follow Jesus, as a disciple you must become like Jesus. Peter explains this process, "Christ...leaving us an example, that you should follow His steps" (1 Pet. 2:21). Therefore, disciple-making grandparents must live like Jesus, so their grandchildren will follow their example and become like Jesus.

A disciple learns to abide in Christ. Not only must a disciple know and become like Christ, they must learn to daily abide in Christ, "I am the vine, you are the branches. He who abides in Me, and I in him, bears much fruit; for without Me you can do nothing" (John 15:5). And what does the word abide mean? It means to *settle down* or to *remain*. So, when you abide in Jesus, you settle down in Him and remain there. Your grandchildren need to see your continual relationship to Christ. You must continually talk to them about Jesus. If they don't come to the house of God on a regular basis, they must see you there when they attend.

A disciple obeys and lives by the Scriptures. Those who are disciples have a passion for the Word of God, and have dedicated themselves to live by the Word of God. "If you abide in My word, you are My disciples indeed. And you shall know the truth, and the truth shall make you free" (John 8:31-32). Have your grandchildren seen you make "hard" decisions to follow Jesus? If yes...good! If no...explain to them how you obey Jesus so they will know you better, and understand your faith better. However, don't live on yesterday's experiences; make Jesus real today. If you are a radical disciple, there'll be tough decisions to make on a continual basis. There is no growth in Christ without change, and there is no change without discarding the old and choosing the new. As you grow daily in the Scriptures, let your grandchildren know what you are learning and how you are growing.

A disciple knows how to pray. It is not enough just to know Christ and to follow Him daily, a disciple must converse with Him each day. You must talk to Him about your needs and desires, "If you abide in Me, and My words abide in you, you will ask what you desire, and it shall be done for you" (John 15:7). The best way to become a disciple-maker of your grandchildren is to pray with them. This can be done at meals, but do more than pray for the food. Find out what's going on in their life, and pray with them about their concerns. When they leave to return home, pray with them about a safe journey, especially if it's a long trip. And don't forget to ask them how you can pray for them while they are away.

A disciple makes Christian love a distinguishing mark of life. A true disciple does not hate, but loves. Sometimes it is difficult for children to obey their parents; because all children think they are justified in their disobedience. However, parents must discipline in love, so they teach their children not only to do the right things, but parents must teach their children to love them, as well as love one another, "A new commandment I give to you, that you love one another; as I have loved you, that you also love one another" (John 13:34). Your life must be characterized by love if you are going to be a radical disciple of Jesus.

A disciple witnesses to unsaved people and serves others. Those who are disciples will share their faith with lost people, both by being a good testimony,

"You shall be witnesses to me" (Acts 1:8) as well as by giving the plan of salvation to them. By serving other people, grandparents demonstrate they are both servants of Jesus Christ, and they follow the example of Christ in their disciple-making role. Grandparents must live as they expect their grandchildren to live, "Greater love has no one than this, than to lay down one's life for his friends" (John 15:13)

HOW DISCIPLE-MAKING GRANDPARENTS DO IT?

Disciple-making by example. Paul told Timothy, "You have carefully followed my doctrine, manner of life, purpose, faith, longsuffering, love, perseverance, persecutions..." (2 Tim. 3:10-11). Timothy knew Paul well. Timothy had heard Paul's sermons, but more importantly, Timothy had seen how Paul responded to opposition. When Paul was physically stoned in Lystra, Timothy saw it all and knew one day he might die a martyr's death. In each and every experience, Timothy learned how to be a disciple of Jesus Christ. As Albert Schweitzer observed, "Example is not the main thing, it is the only thing."

Good parents become disciple-makers by association. That means grandparents must spend time with their grandchildren to influence them for Jesus Christ. And in their relationship, grandparents must demonstrate acceptance, love and a desire for grandchildren to walk with God. Notice how Paul called Timothy, "My beloved son" (2 Tim. 1:2). You can almost feel the passion Paul has for Timothy in his introduction to this letter. Do your grandchildren feel they are "your beloved sons and daughters?"

Grandparents become disciple-makers by assignment. Paul did not want to just tell Timothy lessons or doctrine, rather he put young Timothy to work serving the Lord. Paul sent Timothy to minister in Corinth, Macedonia, Philippi, Thessalonica, etc. When Paul was run out of Thessalonica by a mob that wanted to kill him, Paul left Timothy to preach the Gospel and build up the church. When Paul was in prison in Rome, Timothy was sent to Ephesus to pastor the church in that city. Paul was not afraid to give young Timothy a difficult assignment, probably not just to train Timothy, but to get the work of Christ done. In the same way, you have to give your grandchildren assignments. Can you "bribe" them to learn scripture verses by offering a baked apple pie or whatever they want? Can you financially help them on a student missionary trip to Appalachia or Central America? Can you think of other assignments where your grandchildren could grow in Christ?

Grandparents become disciple-makers by instruction. How did Paul disciple Timothy? Probably through the content of his preaching and teaching. Timothy heard Paul preach publicly and privately, and he learned what discipleship meant in the process. Timothy was not just another face in the crowd. Paul reminded Timothy to pass on the message, "you heard of me" (2 Tim. 2:2). Grandparents will need to take the time and energy to instruct—systematically—the things their grandchildren need to know. Remember some of the greatest lessons are taught in 10 seconds by the "minute-teacher." You can change lives quickly when your lesson meets the desperate need that your grandchild seeks. Also, some lessons may take a lifetime to communicate. Whatever it takes, be ready to do it.

Grandparents become disciple-makers by private counsel. There were probably many intimate conversations between Paul and Timothy that were not written down because they were private. However, we do have their personal correspondence. Paul wrote to Timothy in two letters instructing him about his medical problems (1 Tim. 5:23), telling him not to be bashful and reluctant (1 Tim. 4:12), telling him to stir up his gift (2 Tim. 1:6), telling him to handle older elders in the church (1 Tim. 5:1), telling him how to handle widows and children (1 Tim. 5:3-7), and a number of other personal items. You'll want to counsel your grandchildren when they bring problems to you, and sometimes you'll have to tenderly approach them when they have a problem but are reluctant to approach you. Counsel them! Counseling is problem-solving, counseling is decision-making, counseling is pointing them toward the future.

Grandparents become disciple-makers by encouragement. Notice, Paul was not reluctant to encourage young Timothy. First, he listed Timothy's name with his names six times in the Word of God. This is encouragement by association. Then, Paul publicly expressed appreciation for Timothy (1 Tim. 4:17) and told the Philippians, "For I have no one like-minded (like Timothy) who will sincerely care for your state" (Phil. 2:20). So, what does that mean for grandparents? It's all right to brag about grandchildren, because that's one way of encouraging them, i.e., reinforcing their discipleship to Jesus Christ. When a grandparent tells someone about how their grandchildren follow the Lord—in front of their grandchildren—it may motivate the grandchildren to live up to the expectations of their grandparents.

Grandparents become disciple-makers by prodding. Timothy was reluctant and at times bashful. Timothy probably needed a "jump start" for his ministry. So, Paul told him, "Stir up the gift of God which is in you" (2 Tim. 1:6). Again, he told him, "Be strong" (2 Tim. 2:1), warning him not to give heed to deceiving spirits and doctrines of demons" (1 Tim. 4:1), and "Neglect not the gift that is in you" (1 Tim. 4:14). What does that mean for grandparents? Sometimes you will have to prod your grandchildren into Christian service. This doesn't always mean scolding; it can be an innocent question. "How did you like church?" (That's a sly way of finding out if they went to church). You could ask, "What did you get out of Bible study?" (which is a sly way of finding out if they are reading the scriptures). Also, you could ask, "What is the greatest thing you are praying for? (That's a sly way of finding out if they are praying and trusting God for things in their life). Finally, you can ask, "How can I pray for you?"

PART TWO

50 DAILY DEVOTIONS
Grandparents in the Bible

Section 1

GRANDPARENTS GIVE HERITAGE

THE strongest point in this section is *grandparents give heritage.* There are many types of influences that grandparents have, but perhaps the greatest is they focus on the past and point to the future. This section is based on Second Timothy 2:2 when first-generation Paul influenced second-generation Timothy, who in turn influenced third-generation "faithful men" who influence fourth-generation "others also."

Day 1   Spiritual Grandchildren Prove Your Integrity

Day 2   Pour Your Life into Children and Grandchildren

Day 3   Grandparenting by Example

Day 4   Become Necessary for Them

Day 5   Grandparenting a Second Opportunity

Day 6   Grandparenting With Little Help

Day 7   Follow God in Spite of Parents and Grandparents

Day 1

SPIRITUAL GRANDCHILDREN PROVE YOUR INTEGRITY

"And the things that you have heard from me among many witnesses, commit these to faithful men who will be able to teach others also."

2 Timothy 2:2, NKJV

THERE is a great parallel between becoming a grandparent and being a disciple-maker. The grandparent must first produce children, teach them, and pour their lives into them. Then, the children must marry and have grandchildren. The effectiveness of a parent is measured in their effectiveness to teach the third generation everything that was taught to them by the first generation. This picture of physical reproduction is illustrated in spiritual reproduction. As a first-generation Christian disciple must pass on to the second-generation Christians the task of also being a disciple-maker, so that the third generation of Christians are as strong as the first.

Lord, thank You for my parents and grandparents. May I be faithful to pass on to my children what they taught me. And thank You for my spiritual parents and grandparents. May I be a faithful Christian who passes on to my spiritual children all that was taught to me. Amen.

Just as a Christian must know Christ, follow Him, and be a faithful servant, so spiritual Christians must learn everything about Your faith and then pass on to their spiritual third-generation Christians the faith you poured into them. The future of Christianity hangs on all believers loving Christ, growing in Christ, and serving Christ. Then they must pass on the faith to the next or third generation.

Lord, I want to be as faithful in every way; I will be faithful in learning and growing and serving You. I want to be faithful in pouring my faith into the next generation. I will win people to Christ, I will teach them, be an example to them, and pray for them. May they pass on to the third generation what I have poured into them. Amen.

READING:

2 Timothy 2:1-26

REFLECTION

POUR YOUR LIFE INTO CHILDREN AND GRANDCHILDREN

"As apostles of Christ we certainly had a right to make some demands of you, but instead we were like children among you. Or we were like a mother feeding and caring for her own children. We loved you so much that we shared with you not only God's Good News but our own lives, too."

2 Timothy 2:2, NKJV

GRANDPARENTS can once again experience the miracle of new life. First, they experience the miracle of children being born to them. Then they experience grandchildren being born to their children. When God sculptured Adam out of red mud on the shore of the Euphrates River, he breathed God-life into him, and Adam became a living soul. God gave him a name—as all parents do—calling him Adam meaning *red man*. That life was passed from parent to child until it reached you and me. The miracle continues when we have grandchildren.

Lord, thank You for life that I received from my parents. May I live for You because I am made in Your image (Genesis 2:6 ff). May my children and grandchildren live for You as I have lived for you. I want to glorify You because I am made in Your image. Amen.

Paul talks of his care for his spiritual children in Thessalonians. He loved them as a mother loves her children and gives her life to them. So, Paul's children received the Gospel from Paul, but they also received "his own soul" (v. 8, KJV). In the same way, you must pour your soul into the lives of those you win to Christ.

Lord, thank You for physical life. I dedicate my body to You. Thank You for spiritual life, I yield my whole self to You to glorify and serve You. Fill me with Your spirit, use me. Amen.

READING:

1 Thessalonians 2:1-20

REFLECTION

Day 3

GRANDPARENTING BY EXAMPLE

"But you, Timothy, certainly know what I teach, and how I live, and what my purpose in life is. You know my faith, my patience, my love, and my endurance."

2 Timothy 3:10, NLT

GRANDPARENTS experience more than producing a third generation of physical children. To be a grandparent you see potential in your grandchildren. You are not distracted by the demand of daily necessities and correcting them, and providing shelter, food, clothes, and education for them. A grandparent sees the good things in their grandchildren, and hopefully can do it better the second time around. Grandparents can see the potential in their grandchildren, perhaps more than their parents see or anyone else. That is because grandparents look for their great potential. Grandparents have experience more, so they have the big picture—and perhaps the optimistic picture.

Lord, give me vision to see what could happen in the lives of my children and grandchildren. Then give me grace to see them as You see them. Give me strength to help them. Finally give me the resources to aid them on life's journey. Amen.

You have great dreams for those you win to Christ, just as Paul had for Timothy and the next generations to follow. A grandparent has seen more, experienced more, accomplished more, and been more places. Now in their way, "grand" years, they shall be able to influence their third generation in a "grand" way for their grandchildren.

Lord, give me Your eyes to see my children and grandchildren as You see them. Give me an open heart to go to them and pray for them. Give me strength to do what I have to do. Give me wisdom to pour myself into them. Amen.

READING:

2 Timothy 1:1-7; 4:1-8

REFLECTION

_____

_____

_____

_____

_____

_____

_____

_____

_____

_____

_____

Day 4

BECOME NECESSARY
FOR THEM

*"Grandchildren are the crowning glory of the aged;
parents are the pride of their children."*

Proverbs 17:6, NLT

"May you live to enjoy your grandchildren. May Israel have peace!"

Psalm 128:6, NLT

"The godly walk with integrity; blessed are their children who follow them."

Proverbs 20;7, NLT

A disciple-making grandparent must be a reproduction of reproducers. A parent can rejoice in children, for "children are a heritage from the Lord" (Psalm 127:3). Children bring happiness to the home, "Happy is the man who has his quiver full of them (children)" (Psalm 127:3). Every child who is born has the potential of producing a childlike themselves, and grandchildren like themselves. Therefore, the home is a classroom to teach, train, correct, mold, guide, and energize. Parents can and should teach the necessities of life, but grandparents can help the child fulfill their destiny.

Lord, help me see what my children can do, and help me assist them to realize it. Then help me see the potential of my grandchildren and give me grace and opportunity to energize them to reach their potential. Amen.

Obviously, we reproduce ourselves physically in our children. But what about reproducing ourselves emotionally, spiritually, and socially to make an impact on society and the world. You have done a good job when you reproduce yourself in your children and an outstanding job when you reproduce yourself in your grandchildren.

Lord, give me faith to move mountains (Mark 11:22-24) and help me influence my children to do more for You than I have done. Then Lord, I want to influence my grandchildren to do more for You then I dream. To You be the glory! Amen.

READING:

Psalm 127:1-5;

Psalm 122:1-6;

Proverbs 4:1-27

REFLECTION

_____

_____

_____

_____

_____

_____

_____

_____

Day 5

GRANDPARENTING, A SECOND OPPORTUNITY

"Call me . . .Mara, for the Almighty has made life very bitter for me."

Ruth 1:20, NLT

*"The women said to Naomi...'the Lord has a new provider
a redeemer for your family."*

Ruth 4:14, ELT

WE serve the God of the second chance. Because He is merciful, He will forgive our sins and failures by the blood of Jesus Christ (1 John 1:7). Naomi failed miserably with the first two sons. She took her family out of the influence of Israel and the worship of the true God, exposing them to the idols of Moab. Her sons married outside God's covenant, and they died along with Naomi's husband. But God gave her a second chance through the influence of her daughter-in-law Ruth. The greatest "second Chance" was the privilege of influencing her grandson Obed.

Lord, thank You for Your mercy. I am not perfect, and I have not always made the correct choices. Forgive me...accept me...fill me...use me. Amen.

Naomi failed her first two sons, but God who saw her changed heart, gave her a second chance with her grandson Obed. She took the grandson "and laid it in her bosom" (Ruth 4:16, KJV). She was too old to nurse the baby, but she became his primary influence for God. Obed was grandfather to King David.

Lord, You saw Naomi's heart, whereas I only see the outward actions of people. Thank You for giving Naomi a second change. Continue to give me more opportunities to serve You. Amen.

READING:

Ruth 1:1-22; 4:13-22

REFLECTION

_____

_____

_____

_____

_____

_____

_____

_____

_____

_____

GRANDPARENTS WITH LITTLE HELP

"Train up your child in the way they should live,
and when they are old, they will live that way."

Proverbs 22:6, ELT

SOMETIMES a grandparent doesn't get any help influencing their grandchildren. Lois was a godly grandmother married to a Gentile who apparently gave little influence in the life of his grandson Timothy. Her daughter Eunice also married a Gentile, and again received little help in influencing his son Timothy. But a grandmother in Lystra, a mountain town without synagogue support or another dominate male, have influenced Timothy to serve God with all his heart. Today, if a woman doesn't have the support of a husband to train her son in godliness—what can she do? She can produce a godly grandson like Timothy.

> *Lord, use me to influence my children and grandchildren, even when I have little help.*
> *Help me make a difference so they become godly. Help me influence my children and grand-*
> *children as though I am the only one who can "train up a child in the way he should go"*
> *(Proverbs 22:6). Amen.*

In one sense, every grandmother and mother hold the key to a child's spiritual success. The word *train* means to control or disciple, so the child lives out the way of life determined by parent or grandparent. That means does enough to know them and love them. Does enough to correct wrong actions and model proper actions. Does enough to feel a child's heart obedience, and to pray with them.

Lord, I want to be the greatest influence on my children and grandchildren. I want them to live for Christ like I do, only better Lord, work through me to work in their lives. Amen.

READING:

Acts 16:1-10;

2 Timothy 1:3-7; 3:14-17

REFLECTION

_____

_____

_____

_____

_____

_____

_____

_____

_____

_____

Day 7

FOLLOW GOD IN SPITE OF PARENTS AND GRANDPARENTS

"Asa pleased the Lord by obeying Him, like his great grandfather David."

1 Kings 15:11, ELT

"The Spirit of the Lord spoke through Azariah the prophet...listen to me Asa...the Lord will stay with you as long as you stay with Him!"

2 Chronicles 15:1-2, ELT

ASA'S grandfather Rehoboam and father Abijam compromised with sin, allowed idol worship. His grandmother Maachah was even more evil. Asa "deposed his grandmother Maachah from her position as queen mother...he cut down her obscene Asherah pole" (1 Kings 15:13, NLT). Asa did not follow his parents or grandparents, but "Asa's heart remained completely faithful to the Lord throughout his life" (1 Kings 15:14, NLT).

Lord, thank You that the influence of King David reached over his grandson Rehoboam and great grandson Abijam to capture the heart of Asa. Thank You for each generation that serves You faithfully. Amen.

We really don't know who influenced Asa to follow the Lord. Yet in spite of all the evil around him, Asa was faithful to God. That should motivate us to pray for God to raise up godly leaders—both men and women—who will live godly and led others to live for God.

Lord, I thank You for my godly parents and grandparents. Help me to live as godly as them and give me strength to live above and beyond their standards of living. Amen.

READING:

1 Kings 15:1-23

REFLECTION

Section 2

JACOB

TO outside observers, it seems Jacob was an unlikely son to be used greatly of God. At the beginning he was called "supplanter" or "contender" because Jacob did everything illegal to get the birth right and inheritance from his older brother Esau. But God saw Jacob's unusual motivation and choose him and used him. Even when blessing his grandsons, Jacob chose the second-born Ephraim over the first-born Manasseh. This picture of Jacob blessing his grandsons opens up grandparents to tell their modern grandchildren what God expects of them. It gives them an opportunity to bless their grandchildren.

Day 8

BLESSING A CHILD

"Jacob crossed his arms as he reached out to lay his hands on the boys' heads...'May the God before whom my grandfather Abraham and my father, Isaac, walked...may he bless these boys.'"

Genesis 48:14-16, NLT

WHAT is involved in blessing a child? It is more than money, family articles, or privilege, it is asking God to give the child a spiritual purpose in life and sufficient reasons to carry out that vision. It also involves the spiritual legacy godly parents leave behind. It is a challenge to carry on the torch for God, don't drop it...hide it...don't change it. It involves the challenge to live a moral life in an immoral world. Grandparents can be the spiritual GPS to guide their grandchildren through life when they might not be around.

Lord, help me understand my spiritual responsibly to my children and grandchildren. Help me be strong and not drop the torch, but to past it on to the next generation(s) with authority. Amen.

When you are a grandparent, you can add value to your grandchildren when you pray for them and ask God to do great things for your grandchild—you are lifting the self-perception of what God can do for them. Grandparents can both give their grandchildren a vision of their future; they can also add a little polish and shine it up for them to see it and aspire to it.

Lord, give me a vision of what I should do as an example for my children and grandchildren. Help me understand it...shine it into their lives and give them a desire to do great things for You. Amen.

READING:

Genesis 48:1-22

REFLECTION

Day 9

GOD CHOOSES JACOB

Esau exclaimed, "No wonder his name is Jacob (contender)...
for now he has cheated me twice. First, he took my rights
of first born, and now he has stolen my blessing"

Genesis 27:36, NLT

"God can draw a straight line with a crooked stick."

—Martin Luther

G OD saw something in Jacob that no one else saw, and God chose him and used him greatly. But his ambitions "trick" as a young man got him sent 800 miles away for 20 years. Jacob met God at Luz and renamed it Bethel (house of God). His early physical "aggressiveness" was turned into spiritual aggressiveness. Now Jacob meets his two grandsons and predicts how God will use them in the future. God can transform a brash rebel into a spiritual grandpa.

Lord, thank You for saving me from my sins. I confess them all along with my mistakes and rebellion. Now I testify to all, Jesus as my Lord. I give myself to follow You. May I be a great testimony to my children and grandchildren. Amen.

Jacob's name meant *supplanter* or *contender* as one person contends for the position of another. Jacob who was second born always contended for first; Esau's place. First born gives a person leadership of the family heritage and a double portion of financial inheritance. What Jacob sought by trickery, he later received after meeting God—surrendering to Him. At the end of Jacob's life, he enjoyed both, the spiritual leadership the Jewish family, i.e., children of Israel, and double portion of his prosperity.

Lord, thank You for Jacob's testimony to the world and me. I want to be transformed so I can be used by You. I want to make a spiritual influence on my family. I ask for a double portion of Your blessing. Amen.

READING:

Genesis 25:24-34; 27:1-46

REFLECTION

Day 10

A SPIRITUAL INHERITANCE

"The next morning Jacob got up very early. He took the stone he had rested his head against, and he set it upright as a memorial pillar. Then he poured olive oil over it. He named that place Bethel (which means "house of God"), although it was previously called Luz."

Genesis 28:18-19, NLT

"God Almighty appeared to me...and blessed me."

Genesis 48:3, NLT

WHAT can grandparents give their grandchildren when they don't have much? They can give them a spiritual inheritance. They can put God's name upon them, as well as putting the family's name on them. The most important gift is not money, possessions, or even property. The most important thing is a spiritual heritage to guide the lives of their grandchildren. Jacob told of meeting God at Bethel where his life was changed.

Lord, thank You for my spiritual heritage. You met me and saved me. I will tell my children and/grandchildren what You did for me and what You can do for them. Amen.

It was important for Jacob to give his grandchildren his testimony of what God did in his life. It is like you today telling your children and grandchildren your testimony of salvation and how God led you...provided for you...and protected you. The most life-changing experience was when you met Jesus Christ and He saved you.

Lord, thank You for transforming my life. That is the most important thing that has ever happened in my life. I will tell all my relatives how You saved me, changed me, and gave me direction to live. Amen.

READING:

Genesis 28:1-22

REFLECTION

Day 11

A SPIRITUAL VISION

"He (God) said to me, 'I will make you fruitful, and I will multiply your descendants. I will make you a multitude of nations. And I will give this land of Canaan to your descendants after you as an everlasting possession. Now I am claiming as my own sons these two boys of yours, Ephraim and Manasseh.'"

Genesis 48:4-5, NLT

THE greatest gift you can give your children/grandchildren is a spiritual vision of what God can do for them. Jacob knew what God had done for him, now he passes on to the two boys their spiritual inheritance. Much of God's original promise to Abraham was repeated to the boys. In a real sense you must challenge your children/grandchildren to believe in Christ...follow Him...be faithful and obedient.

Lord, thank You for saving me. I will pass on to my children and grandchildren the great things You have done for me. I pray for them, that they would love Jesus...follow Him and be obedient to Him. Amen.

Jacob didn't have a Bible, he quoted from memory the Abrahamic Covenant. That means both Abraham and Isaac had passed on what God told them. You must do the same, pass on to your children/grandchildren what God has done for you. Remember children like to hear stories from a grandparent. Remind them of God's faithfulness. "May the God before whom my grandfather Abraham and my father, Isaac, walked—the God who has been my shepherd all my life, to this very day...bless these boys" (Genesis 48:15-16, NLT).

Lord, thank You for transforming my life. That is the most important thing that has ever happened in my life. I will tell all my relatives how You saved me, changed me, and gave me direction to live. Amen.

READING:

Genesis 48:1-22

REFLECTION

BLESSING YOUR GRANDCHILDREN

"Then he positioned the boys in front of Jacob. With his right hand he directed Ephraim toward Jacob's left hand, and with his left hand he put Manasseh at Jacob's right hand...May the God before whom my grandfather Abraham and my father, Isaac, walked...bless those boys."

Genesis 48:13, 15-16, NLT

NOTICE the way Jacob blessed his grandchildren. He "kissed and embraced them" (Genesis 48:10). Then Jacob placed his hands on their heads, which is symbolic of passing yourself to them. God loves symbols, whether it is the symbol of baptism or The Lord's Table. Your hand on your grandchildren's head shows you approve them. It is also a picture of your life flowing into their life. As you read the text, notice Jacob blessed the younger first, just as God had blessed him the second born. Esau, his brother was the first born.

Lord, my prayer is for You to bless my children and grandchildren. But I will go the next step, I will place my hands on their heads asking You to bless them as You have blessed me. Then Lord, I will ask You to bless them "exceedingly, abundantly, above all I ask" (Ephesians 3:20). Amen.

Remember, Jacob gave them his name, "Let my name be upon them"(v. 5). You want to bless your children both naturally and supernaturally. That means you will do financial things for them, give to them, and provide for them in any way you are able. Spiritually, you will testify your faith to them and teach them so they will be influenced by God. Think of all the things God has given you, and the places God has led you, and the lessons God has taught you. Your children and grandchildren won't know them unless you teach them.

Lord, I will bless my children and grandchildren financially, as best I can. Then I will bless them spiritually as best I can. Amen.

READING:

Genesis 48:1-22

REFLECTION

_____

_____

_____

_____

_____

_____

_____

_____

_____

_____

Day 13

PASSING IT ON

"Behold, I the Lord will prosper you in all that you do. I will give you many children, and you will become a great nation. I the Lord promise this land to you—a promised land—that you shall inherit this land for an everlasting possession."

Adapted from Genesis 48:4

GOD gave Jacob the fourfold promise of blessings. He passed it to his grandsons: (1) God's prosperity, (2) many children, (3) a great nation, (4) the Promised Land. The promise was given first to Abraham, then Isaac, and Jacob was third in line. The two boys—Manasseh and Ephraim—were the fourth generation. What generation is your spiritual heritage? Each one is important, for if you didn't receive what is given to you and pass it on to the next generation—then the blessing of God is thwarted, Jacob shared what God expected of him, and he passed it on to his grandsons what God expected of them.

Lord, help me realize the importance of passing on to my children and grandchildren all the lessons and expectations You have given me. I pray for the next generation. May Your work continue beyond my limited scope and perception. Amen.

Grandmothers are just as important as grandfathers. Jacob told the boys about their grandmother: (1) she died in travel, (2) he was there when she died, (3) they were almost home, (4) she was buried by the road (Genesis 48:7). The love and care of one grandparent for the other should be extended to the grandchildren.

Lord, thank You for children and grandchildren. I pray they would love and follow You as deeply as I. But I ask for Your special work in their lives so they will go beyond me in love and service to You. Amen.

READING:

Genesis 48:7; Genesis 35:1-20

REFLECTION

Day 14

SEEING THE FUTURE

"So, Jacob set out for Egypt with all his possessions. And when he came to
Beersheba, he offered sacrifices to the God of his father, Isaac. During the
night God spoke to him in a vision. 'Jacob! Jacob!' he called.
'Here I am,' Jacob replied. 'I am God, the God of your father,'
the voice said. 'Do not be afraid to go down to Egypt,
for there I will make your family into a great nation.'"

Genesis 46:1-3, NLT

JACOB spent the last part of his life living for God. Early on he thought his son Joseph was killed by wild animals, and he mourned for him for years. But in the plan of God, Joseph was sent to Egypt to save the world from the coming famines. Now toward the end of his life, Jacob goes to Egypt to see Joseph. God appears to Jacob in a dream to reassure him that in Egypt the nation of Israel will become large and powerful. Also, God promised to not only take the children of Abraham to Egypt, He will bring them back.

Lord, thank You for reassuring Jacob of Your plan for his life and for Your people. I thank
You for having a plan for my life (Jeremiah 29:11). I want to find Your plan for my life and
do it. I want Your blessings on all I do. Amen.

Jacob got to bless Pharaoh (Genesis 47:1-9) and bless his grandchildren. Remember the blessing on others (including grandchildren) is important because it tells them what the Lord will do for them and what they are to do in serving Him. Even in blessing his grandchildren, Jacob blessed the grandson born second, just as Jacob who also was born second in his family, got the primary blessing.

Lord, I want Your best blessing on my life, no matter in what order I was born in my family. In the same way, I want Your blessing on my children and grandchildren. I will faithfully serve You, just as I pray, they will also serve You. Amen.

READING:

Genesis 47:1-9, 48:1-22

REFLECTION

_____

_____

_____

_____

_____

_____

_____

_____

_____

_____

Section 3

NAOMI

THE story begins telling how Naomi and her husband left the Promised Land where Jehovah was worshiped and the Ten Commandments were the foundation of its civilization, to go live in Moab, a culture based in idol worship. They sought wealth and security in a time of famine. Naomi's husband died. Her two sons married Gentile wives, and shortly thereafter they also died. God gave her second chance when she returned to Bethlehem with her daughter-in-law Ruth.

Ruth married Boaz and her son Obed was in the line of Messiah, and the future grandfather of King David. Grandmother Naomi was given the task of raising young Obed, and through this opportunity a compromising mother became a godly grandmother.

Day 15   Grandchildren Give Purpose

Day 16   Restorer of Life

Day 17   A Second Chance

Day 18   Show Me Your Repentance

Day 19   Importance of Grandmothers

Day 20   Give Grandchildren the Best of Your Life

Day 21   Grandchildren May Be Your Second Chance

GRANDCHILDREN GIVE PURPOSE

"Things are far more bitter for me than for you,
because the Lord himself has raised his fist against me."

Ruth 1:13, NLT

"May he (Obed) restore your youth."

Ruth 4:15, NLT

NAOMI did it all wrong the first time. She and her husband focused on money during the famine. She did not do a good job with her sons. They married outside the Jewish faith. She lost her husband, her sons...everything. But God did not let her suffer the consequences for the rest of her life. God (the One of second chances) gave her a second opportunity. Just as grandchildren give energy to grandparents today. She directed Ruth properly, and God gave her a grandson—Obed. His name meant "worshiper."

Lord, thank You for giving Naomi a second change to serve You and she did. Thank You
for Obed, grandfather to King David. We see Your mercy in Naomi's second chance. Amen.

Naomi could look all the way back to Rahab to see the mercy of God giving the prostitute a second chance both spiritually and physically. When Jericho was destroyed, Rahab and her family were saved.

But more than that, Rahab is in the line of the Messiah (Matthew 1:5). God continually displays His mercy to those who call to Him.

Lord, thank You for forgiving me each time I messed up. I worship You for Your grace and mercy. I will tell my children and grandchildren how You have been so gracious to me. Amen.

READING:

Ruth 1:1-22;

Joshua 2:1-21

REFLECTION

Day 16

RESTORER OF LIFE

"Ruth...bare a son. And the women said to Naomi,
'Blessed be the Lord'. . . he shall be to thee a restorer of life."

Ruth 4:13-15, KJV

ONE of the great challenges to grandparents who reach retirement, is to focus on their grandchildren. Retirement is traditionally considered playing shuffleboard...or fishing... or puttering around the house. But Naomi's life was restored in her grandson Obed. The grandson gave new purpose to Naomi. She became the boy's nursemaid, "Naomi took the baby and cuddled him to her breast" (Ruth 4:16). Even the women in the community could see the difference. It was these friends who said, Obed, "restored her life." What would it take to restore your life?

Lord, thank You for this family story to tell me how You prepared for Jesus Christ coming into the world. Thank You for giving Naomi a second chance. Thank You for her opportunity to influence Obed—who influenced King David. Amen.

Grandchildren revitalize the life of their grandparents, whether they run through the house, or constantly talk, or get into everything. If you are a grandparent, you get the privilege of looking back at your heritage and looking through your grandchildren's eyes to see the future. Make sure you influence their young eyes to look both to the past and present—to see what you see. If you don't tell them, they won't know.

Lord, thank You for my parents and grandparents. Help me continue to learn from them. Thank You for grandchildren. Help me to focus their eyes to see what I have seen and what I see coming. Amen.

READING:

Ruth 4:1-22

REFLECTION

Day 17

A SECOND CHANCE

"And Ruth said, Intreat me not to leave thee, or to return from following after thee: for whither thou goest, I will go; and where thou lodgest, I will lodge: thy people shall be my people, and thy God my God."

Ruth 1:16, KJV

PARENTS can do a terrible job raising their children, but God can give them a second chance with grandchildren. Naomi left the land of promise when God dwelt in the temple in Jerusalem to live in a land of idols. She left the fellowship and influences of God's people to live with the unsaved in Moab. She ran away from her problems (famine) seeking an easy life. Even when she realized her punishment was from God (1:20), she counseled Ruth to return to the old life and Moab's gods (1:15). Yet God in His mercy gave Naomi a second chance through her grandson, Obed (4:16).

Lord, thank You for giving Naomi a second chance to serve You. Thank You for Your kindness to me on many occasions. I will determine to serve You with all my heart. Amen.

Naomi made a terrible blunder. When Orpah started to return to her old life in Moab, Naomi told Ruth, "Thy sister-in-law is gone back unto her people and unto her gods: return thou after thy sister-in-law" (1:15, KJV). Naomi thought only of herself, not what was best for Ruth. Here the faith of Ruth stood out, when she said, "Intreat me not to leave thee, or to return from following thee...thy people shall be my people and thy God, my God" (1:16, KJV). The faith of Ruth eventually brought blessings into the life of Naomi.

Lord, help me always make decisions by faith. Help me always see Your salvation to my problems, and the possibility of Your blessings on my life. Like Ruth, "I will not leave Thee, or return from following Thee." Amen.

READING:

Ruth 1:1-22

REFLECTION

Day 18

SHOW ME YOUR REPENTANCE

*"And Ruth said, Intreat me not to leave thee, or to return from following after
thee: for whither thou goest, I will go; and where thou lodgest, I will lodge:
thy people shall be my people, and thy God my God. Where thou diest, will I die."*

Ruth 1:16-17, KJV

NAOMI'S repentance is seen in her actions. She recognized God's punishment for going to a heathen culture to live. She admitted, "The Almighty has sent such tragedy" (Ruth 1:21, LB). Next, Naomi guided Ruth to Israel's spiritual heritage (2:1-3). Then, Naomi directed Ruth toward family and spiritual redemption (2:19-22). And finally, as the relationship developed between Ruth and Boaz, she counseled Ruth to have patience and trust the situation to develop. "Sit still my daughter...for the man will not rest until he has concluded the matter this day" (3:18).

Lord, thank You for the wise counsel of Naomi; and the willingness of Ruth to serve You. Give me patience when to rest and give me strength when I need actions to carry out Your will. Amen.

After Ruth and Boaz were married, God gave them a son. The women of the community were excited and recognized the influence Naomi had in making it happen. The women of the community yelled, "Blessed *be* the Lord...may his name be famous in Israel! (4:14). His name was Obed, derived from a Hebrew word meaning "servant" and tied to "worship." The child would serve the Lord with worship.

Lord, I worship You for saving me and leading me to this hour. I praise You for Your power to work through my family and circumstances to bring me to this hour. I want to be like Obed, I want to worship You. Amen.

READING:

Ruth 4:1-22

REFLECTION

Day 19

IMPORTANCE OF
GRANDMOTHERS

*"Don't call me Naomi," she responded. 'Instead, call me Mara, for the Almighty
has made life very bitter for me. I went away full, but the Lord has brought me
home empty. Why call me Naomi when the Lord has caused me to suffer
and the Almighty has sent such tragedy upon me?'"*

Ruth 1:20-21, KJV

NAOMI'S repentance is seen in her actions. She recognized God's punishment for going
to a heathen culture to live. She admitted, "The Almighty has sent such tragedy" (Ruth
1:21, LB). Next, Naomi guided Ruth to Israel's spiritual heritage (2:1-3). Then, Naomi
directed Ruth toward family and spiritual redemption (2:19-22). And finally, as the relationship
developed between Ruth and Boaz, she counseled Ruth to have patience and trust the situation to
develop. "Sit still my daughter...for the man will not rest until he has concluded the matter this day"
(3:18).

*Lord, thank You for the wise counsel of Naomi; and the willingness of Ruth to serve You.
Give me patience when to rest and give me strength when I need actions to carry out Your
will. Amen.*

After Ruth and Boaz were married, God gave them a son. The women of the community were
excited and recognized the influence Naomi had in making it happen. The women of the community
yelled, "Blessed *be* the Lord...may his name be famous in Israel! (4:14). His name was Obed, derived

from a Hebrew word meaning "servant" and tied to "worship." The child would serve the Lord with worship.

Lord, I worship You for saving me and leading me to this hour. I praise You for Your power to work through my family and circumstances to bring me to this hour. I want to be like Obed, I want to worship You. Amen.

READING:

Ruth 4:1-22

REFLECTION

_____

_____

_____

_____

_____

_____

_____

_____

_____

_____

Day 20

GIVE GRANDCHILDREN THE BEST OF YOUR LIFE

"You must love the Lord your God with all your heart...commit yourselves wholeheartedly to these...repeat them again and again to your children."

Deuteronomy 6:5-7, NLT

GRANDPARENTS have the advantage of both natural and spiritual experiences and *stuff*. Yes, they are spiritual and wise. But when you walk through their home you see an accumulation of trinkets, souvenirs, mementos, and oh yes pictures...lots of pictures. These represent all the experiences God has given them. Scrapbooks are much more than accumulation of photos, they are the accumulation of living long, doing many things, and learning from many experiences. Now, it is their responsibilities to not just give children and grandchildren things, they must communicate vision to the grandchildren and God's plan in their life. Challenge them what God can do for them.

Lord, help me to remember all the lessons You have taught me, so I can tell my children and grandchildren. Help me remember dreams, victories and oh yes, I will tell them what I have learned from my failures. Amen.

Grandchildren need many things from their grandparents. But most of all grandchildren need to see how God has worked in their lives. They need to learn from the failures of parents and grandparents, so they don't do the same things. Give your best to them for the rest of your life, and for the rest of their life.

Lord, help me remember all the lessons You have taught me. Then help me share them with my children and grandchildren. Lord, use me to indelibly influence the lives of my children and grandchildren. Amen.

READING:

Psalm 127;

Deuteronomy 6:6-25

REFLECTION

_____

_____

_____

_____

_____

_____

_____

_____

_____

_____

Day 21

GRANDCHILDREN MAY BE
YOUR SECOND CHANCE

*"Naomi took the baby and cuddled him to her breast. And she cared for him
as if he were her own. The neighbor women said, 'Now at last Naomi has a son
again!' And they named him Obed. He became the father of
Jesse and the grandfather of David."*

Ruth 4:16-17, NLT

NAOMI and her husband did not do it right the first time. They did not raise their sons in godly Bethlehem, but took them to Moab, an idol worshiping nation. Their two sons married outside the faith—they married foreign wives. It looks like they messed up and there was no chance of setting the record straight. Sometimes grandparents have prodigal children to care for. But God gave Naomi a second chance after her husband and both sons died. God gave her Ruth. Look beyond the outward appearance of Ruth to see her heart. She was beautiful on the inside.

*Lord, thank You for giving Ruth to Naomi. The two women were used to help influence
King David. Lord, may I see the future through Your eyes, may I plan my future with Your
guidance. Amen.*

Naomi could look all the way back to Rahab (in the line of Boaz). Naomi could tell stories to Obed how God's grace forgave Rahab the harlot and used her to help God's people. Then Naomi could tell the story of how God's mercy directed her and Ruth to the field of Obed's father. Surely God's provision is seen in the way families come together to carry out God's purpose.

Lord, I want You to work in my family the same way You worked in Naomi's family. Show Your mercy and forgiveness to my family and may we all surrender to You to be used for Your glory. Amen.

READING:

Ruth 4:1-21

REFLECTION

Section 4

ASA

GOD promised David that his sons would be king to rule God's people. But the next three generations did not follow David's example, nor did they fulfill God's expectation that the nation would wholly follow righteousness. David's son Solomon married foreign women who turned his heart from following God. The next son Rehoboam also permitted idol worship as did the next son Abijam. Then young Asa was born into this compromising line, but he identified with godly David, not his father, grandfather, or great grandfather. Notice how Asa is aligned with David, "Asa did what was pleasing in the Lord's sight, as his ancestor David had done" (1 Kings 15:11, NLT).

Asa is a picture of a youth turning against the ungodly examples of men and women in his family to seek the heart of God and follow Him. The great conflict was Asa removing his grandmother Maachah from being queen mother because of her idols and Asherah pole.

Asa was a *revival* king because he changed the law of idols, and he reintroduced worship in the temple and commanded the people to serve the Lord (2 Chronicles 14:4).

Day 22   Ungodly Parents and Grandparents

Day 23   Standing up

Day 24   Call on God

Day 25   Prepare for the Future

Day 26   Asa Was an Exception

Day 27   Revival Results

Day 28   What Brings Revival?

Day 22

UNGODLY PARENTS AND GRANDPARENTS

"He (Abijam) committed the same sins as his father before him, and he was not faithful to the Lord his God, as his ancestor David had been. But for David's sake, the Lord his God...gave Abijam a son to rule after him in Jerusalem."

1 Kings 15:3-4, NLT

GRANDFATHER King Rehoboam sinned and let the people follow a path to evil. His son Abijam continued the downward path. But his small son Asa growing up in the palace saw the abuses and knew the abuses were wrong. Asa became the first revival king. Almost immediately upon becoming king, Asa began cleaning the temple (2 Chronicles 14:3). Apparently, the child saw the abuses of his father and grandfather, not to mention the terrible sins of his grandmother Maachah (daughter of David's rebellious son, Absalom).

Lord, I pray for children who have ungodly parents and grandparents. Help children see the evil of those who lived before them and give the next generation a passion to live right and follow You. Amen.

Asa was 17 years old when his grandfather died, and 20 years old when his father died (1 Kings 15:2). As a young leader he demanded the nation to turn back to God. "He commanded the people of Judah to seek the Lord, their God...to obey his law and his commands" (2 Chronicles 14:4). That is a great start, i.e., returning to the Word of God. That is also, the same place for you to get close to God and follow Him.

Lord, I repent of being lax in learning and knowing Your Scriptures. Forgive me...help me...I will hide Your Word in my heart (Psalm 119:11). I want revival in my life, just as Asa brought revival to God's people. Amen.

READING:

1 Kings 15:1-15;

2 Chronicles 14:1-15

REFLECTION

_____

_____

_____

_____

_____

_____

_____

_____

_____

_____

Day 23

STANDING UP

*"Asa did what was pleasing in the Lord's sight, as his ancestor David had done.
He banished the male and female shrine prostitutes from the land
and got rid of all the idols his ancestors had made."*

1 Kings 15:11-12, NLT

ASA'S grandmother was rebellious Maachah, the daughter of rebellious Absalom who tried to overthrow and kill his father, David the king. Absalom and his daughter Maachah also never lived by God's rules. She created idols and worshipped them. She named her son Abijam (son of Jam, the idol, 1 Kings 15:1), but he also had a Hebrew name, Abijah (2 Chronicles 14:21, son of Jehovah). The grandson Asa saw the evil of his grandmother and determined to serve Jehovah. He led Israel in revival. The people "entered into a covenant to seek the Lord God... with all their hearts...souls" (2 Chronicles 15:9, KJV).

> *Lord, thank You for Your grace to raise up a godly leader—little Asa—in spiritually desperate times. Do it again. Raise up pastors, political leaders, and a revival movement to sweep our nation. I want a revival, like the one that swept Judah under Asa's leadership. Amen.*

Maachah not only gave her son an evil name, she had an evil idol in her garden. There were idols and homosexuals in the temple, plus idolatry all over the land. The original language suggests her idol was a female god. When Asa become king, he, "deposed his grandmother Maachah from her position as queen mother because she had made an obscene Asherah pole" (1 Kings 15:13, NLT). It takes great conviction to go against your parents and grandparents, but Asa was God's man. "Asa's heart remained faithful to the Lord throughout his life" (1 Kings 15:14).

Lord, give me the conviction of Asa to stand up for Your cause and to stand against unrighteousness. Forgive me when I have not done it in the past. Give me strength to always be faithful. Amen.

READING:

2 Chronicles 14:21-15:8

REFLECTION

_____

_____

_____

_____

_____

_____

_____

_____

_____

Day 24

CALL ON GOD

"Then Asa cried out to the Lord his God, "O Lord, no one but you can help the powerless against the mighty! Help us, O Lord our God, for we trust in you alone. It is in your name that we have come against this vast horde. O Lord, you are our God; do not let mere men prevail against you!"

2 Chronicles 14:11, NLT

ASA brought revival to God's people, but quickly the satanic enemy brought the Ethiopian nation against them. There were 300,000 soldiers in Judah, but the enemy had one million warriors and 300 chariots. The odds were overwhelming, so Asa called on Jehovah, "No one but You can help the powerless against the mighty" (v. 11). He pleaded God's name and asked that the enemy not "prevail against You." Did you see Asa's plea? He said the enemy was fighting God, not just the nation of Judah. Are you so identified with God's side, so that when the enemy attacks, you can plead that the attack against you is really against God? Getting on God's side is the basis for victory.

Lord, I confess that sometimes I battle evil opponents by myself, and I forget about You. You remind me it is not my job to seek victory by myself. Teach me the secret of victory in my getting on Your side. Amen.

When the Ethiopians came against God's people, Asa called on God for help. He had no other option. When you get in a hard spot, call on God for deliverance, or for a solution. "In the time of trouble, He should hide me...mine head shall be lifted up over mine enemies" (Psalm 27:5-6, KJV). Remember, it is God who gives the victory.

Lord, I have called upon You for small problems and You have delivered me. Now, I will call upon You when big problems come. Teach me yieldedness to You...faith in You... and Your power. Amen.

READING:

2 Chronicles 14:1-13

REFLECTION

_____

_____

_____

_____

_____

_____

_____

_____

_____

_____

Day 25

PREPARE FOR THE FUTURE

*"So, Asa's kingdom enjoyed a period of peace. During those peaceful years, he was
able to build up the fortified towns...no one tried to make war against him
at this time, for the Lord was giving him rest from his enemies."*

2 Chronicles 14:5-6, NLT

NOT only did Asa destroy the evil infrastructure of idol worship in the kingdom, the young king gave attention to military fortifications. "He built fortified cities in Judah...for he had no war in these years, because the Lord gave him rest" (2 Chronicles 14:6). The principle is to strengthen yourself in peaceful times, because eventually evil will return to attack. It is the Sabbath principle; God gives you one day out of seven to strengthen yourself to go live for Him (or fight for Him) in the rest of the week.

*Lord, thank You for times of rest in my life. I will strengthen myself in prayer, the Word of
God, and Christian fellowship. I will be prepared for the next attack that is coming for it
will surely come. Amen.*

But Asa did more than fortify his defensive walls. "Asa cried to the Lord" (2 Chronicles 14:11), when attacks came. The same is true in your Christian life. The better you equip yourself to serve the Lord in easy times, the easier it is for God to answer in the hard times. We know that hard times are coming, we don't know when, or where; so, let's prepare in easy times. Then we can better face the bad times.

Lord, my life seems to go from one high (easy time) to a low (hard time). Help me get ready for the coming evil days. Thank You for each enjoyable day You give me. Amen.

READING:

2 Chronicles 15:1-19

REFLECTION

Day 26

ASA WAS AN EXCEPTION

"Asa did what was pleasing and good in the sight of the Lord his God."

2 Chronicles 14:2, NLT

"Where sin abounded, grace did much more abound."

Romans 5:20, KJV

THE old saying, *like father like son,* has some exceptions. Asa saw the results of his grandfather Rehoboam's compromise, and the result of his father's weakness. Asa grew up to oppose the evil of his parents. There are always exceptions to the law *like produces like.* In his childhood, "there was no peace to those who went out...but great turmoil" (2 Chronicles 15:5-6). Somewhere in young Asa's mind he determined to follow God. If there was a strong nurse in the palace, or a relative who stood for righteousness—we don't know. But God...it is always God who intervenes in the affairs of life to work His will. But God...was there for Asa.

Lord, thank You for this boy who was true to You. Thank You for my relatives who influenced me to godliness. Thank You for teachers, church workers, or pastors; thank You for all those who influenced my life. Amen.

It is hard for a child to deal with the sins of his parents. But Asa at 21 years of age deposed his grandmother, Maachah, and destroyed her idolatry. He cleansed the temple and instituted reform throughout the nation. "Where sin abounded, grace abounded much more" (Romans 5:20). Where sin abounded in Rehoboam and Abijah, grace abounded much more in Asa.

Lord, thank You for Your grace to me. You know me and You know my parents... thank You for leading me to this hour. May I be strong in the face of sin and compromise. May I be tender and submissive to Your Word. I want to be Your follower. Amen.

READING:

1 John 1:1-10;

Romans 5:15-21

REFLECTION

Day 27

REVIVAL RESULTS

"Asa called together all the people...they sacrificed to the Lord...they entered into a covenant to seek the LORD...with all their hearts... and they found Him, and the Lord gave them rest."

2 Chronicles 15:9, 11, 15, NLT

REVIVAL is only the beginning. Throughout history, great revivals resulted in renewed ministry for God, a stronger church, and many lost people saved. God sent revival to His people through Asa (revival is God pouring Himself on His people). Asa's compromising father and grandfather were gone. Temple sacrifices were restored, and the people repented of their sins, and sought God with all their hearts. God saw their repentance and heard their prayers. The nation had peace. It is the same in your life when you put away sin, return to God, and seek Him with all your heart, He gives you inner joy and peace.

Lord, thank You for Your faithfulness to reward those who seek You with all their heart. I want Your presence in my life. Come sit on the throne of my life and rule all I do. Amen.

One of the outcomes of revival was, "all in Judah were happy" (v. 15). Why? Because "they entered into it with all their heart" (v. 15). Their happiness was not just outward, it was inward spiritual joy. "They earnestly sought after God, and they found Him" (v. 15). Have you found God in all the things you seek in life? Real joy is in Jesus Christ.

Lord, I come seeking Your presence. I want to know You (Philippians 3:10-14), worship You and enjoy Your presence. As I search for You...reveal Yourself to me and bless me with Your presence. Amen.

READING:

2 Chronicles 15:1-19

REFLECTION

Day 28

WHAT BRINGS REVIVAL?

"When Asa heard this message...he took courage and removed all the detestable idols from the land of Judah...he repaired the altar of the Lord which stood in front...of the Lord's Temple."

2 Chronicles 15:8, NLT

REVIVAL is when God pours His presence on His people. Asa took the initiative and led his people in a national revival. It begins when the man of God—the prophet Azariah—preached God's Word. "Seek Him you will find Him. But if you abandoned Him, He will abandon you" (v. 2). Yes, godly Asa led revival, but it was the man of God who preached revival. "For a long time, Israel was without...a priest to teach them and the law to instruct them" (v. 3). God always looks for a man or woman (remember Deborah) to preach revival to His people.

Lord, thank You for reviving Your church in the past...please do it again. Send revival to my church and to my family and begin with me. I repent of sin and I turn to You. Forgive me...accept me...fill me...revive me. Amen.

Don't forget, revival begins in the home and in your heart. Asa had to clean up his family. "King Asa even deposed his grandmother Maachah from...queen mother because she had made an obscene Asherah pole" (v. 16). After that revival spread to the whole nation. What do you have to do to bring revival? What could happen to your family...church...or your neighborhood if God poured Himself into your life?

Lord, I want revival, but more than the outward experience of revival, family, or church; Lord, I want Your presence in my life... I want Your power...I want what revival brings. Amen.

READING:

2 Chronicles 15:1-19

REFLECTION

_____

_____

_____

_____

_____

_____

_____

_____

_____

_____

_____

Section 5

NOAH

THE Bible shows how Noah was God's man to save God's plan for humanity on the earth. "It was by faith that Noah built a large boat to save his family from the flood. He obeyed God, who warned him about things that had never happened before" (Hebrews 11:1, NLT). Yet at the end of his life he got drunk and was a terrible example to his grandson Canaan. Noah is a challenge to all grandparents to be faithful to God from the beginning of life until dearth.

Day 29

NOAH'S FAITH

"It was by faith that Noah built a large boat to save his family from the flood. He obeyed God, who warned him about things that had never happened before. By his faith Noah condemned the rest of the world, and he received the righteousness that comes by faith."

Hebrews 11:7, NLT

WHAT do we know about Noah? The Bible describes him, "Noah was a righteous man, the only blameless person living on earth at the time, and he walked in close fellowship with God" (Genesis 6:9, NLT). Noah heard and saw God who warned him of coming judgment, and God showed him things not yet seen (Hebrews 11:7). Many people see, and hear what God says in the Bible, but do little. Noah acted and began to build a giant boat, 450 feet long (1 ½ times as long as a football field), and three stories tall. How many years did it take Noah and his three sons to build a boat that large? Would you have faith to work that long and that diligently on a project for God?

Lord, thank You for Noah's faith to obey You to build a boat that large and sturdy. Give me that kind of faith to serve You as long as Noah, and to serve as diligently as Noah. Amen.

Faith comes from the Word of God (Romans 10:17). "By faith Noah" (Hebrews 11:7). Noah got his faith from the actual words spoken to him by God (Hebrews 11:13-16). So, faith begins with belief in the Person of God, and grows by obedience to what God commands. Today, you can have the faith of Noah when you see God in Scriptures and obey what God says to you in His word.

Lord, I ask for the faith of Noah. Give me vision of faith to see Your commands in Scriptures. Then give me strength of faith to obey. I want to please You in all ways. Therefore, I will learn Your Words and apply them to my life. Amen.

READING:

Genesis 6:1-22;

Hebrews 11:1-7

REFLECTION

_____

_____

_____

_____

_____

_____

_____

_____

_____

_____

_____

Day 30

SAFE

"But as the days of Noah were, so also will the coming of the Son of Man be.
For as in the days before the flood, they were eating and drinking,
marrying and giving in marriage, until the day that Noah entered
the ark, and did not know until the flood came and took them
all away, so also will the coming of the Son of Man be."

Matthew 24:37-39, NKJV

THE conditions when Jesus returns to judge the earth will be similar to the days before Noah entered his boat. There was no thought of God, but Noah a "preacher of righteousness" (2 Peter 2:5), warned them that God would punish their wickedness (Genesis 6:4-8). The unsaved were warned of their drinking (Matthew 24:38), violence (Genesis 6:13), and unrestrained sin (Genesis 6:5). But it was more than Noah's sermons, the giant boat he was building was a sermon. Noah predicted rain, but it had never rained, only midst watered everything (Genesis 2:5-6). The unsaved today doesn't believe Jesus will return, just as the unsaved didn't believe Noah's preaching.

Lord, I believe what You said in Scripture. It happened in Noah's day just as You said, and it will happen when Jesus comes, just as You said. Help me get all my family in the ark—in Christ—where they will be safe. Amen.

When the boat (ark) was ready, God invited, "Come you and all your family" (Genesis 7:1). Note, God was on the board. When Noah and his family entered, it's a picture of our entering Jesus Christ for safety. Jesus gave us the picture, "you in Me, and I in you" (John 14:20). Only those in Christ, or in the boat, are saved. Are you and your family safely in?

Lord, I have entered Jesus Christ and I am safe from punishment. I also use the word saved.
I am saved from sin and hell because I am in Christ and He dwells in me. Amen.

READING:

Genesis 7:1-24;

John 14:19-21

REFLECTION

Day 31

HOUSEHOLD FAITH

"It was by faith that Noah built a large boat to save his family from the flood. He obeyed God, who warned him about things that had never happened before. By his faith Noah condemned the rest of the world, and he received the righteousness that comes by faith."

Hebrews 11:7, NLT

DO you have household-faith? Noah believed God so deeply that his wife and three sons believed with him that God was going to judge the world. Noah believed it was his task, with the help of his family—to build a giant boat, 450 feet long and 3 stories tall. Noah's faith in God was evidently so real that his three sons, and three daughters-in-law helped prepare the ark. Are all members of your family saved? Noah's household faith was so deep and genuine that his wife and children all saw it... experienced it...and joined with him in saving faith. Who warned you about the Second Coming of Jesus? Have you warned anyone lately?

Lord, I believe in coming judgment, just as Noah believed in a coming flood. Noah did something about it. Lord, I too will do something about Jesus' Second Coming. I will warn people today, and if they don't know what to do about, I will tell them about Jesus. Amen.

What happened to Noah because he believed and obeyed? In the flood he lost everything in the world. The only thing he kept was those with him on the boat. One day you will lose all your property, wealth and possessions—everything. What then? Noah stepped on to the boat losing everything in the flood. Remember, he had everything he needed in the ark. Everything was his, all he had to do was possess it. One day you will leave everything on earth and step into heaven. Then everything will be yours.

Lord, forgive me for holding on to my possession, and real estate and bank accounts. I give You control of it all. Help me use everything for Your glory to get others to believe in Jesus Christ. Amen.

READING:

Genesis 7:1-24;

John 14:19-21

REFLECTION

Day 32

FAITH'S FORESIGHT

"It was by faith that Noah built a large boat to save his family from the flood. He obeyed God, who warned him about things that had never happened before. By his faith Noah condemned the rest of the world, and he received the righteousness that comes by faith."

Hebrews 11:7, NLT

NOAH did not wait until it started to rain to begin building the boat. It took *insight-faith* to build a 3-story ark that is 450 feet long. What does this tell us about faith? The future will be too late to prepare your faith to obey God. *Immediate-faith* begins building a boat that will take 120 years to finish. He had *future-faith* that made him work immediately to prepare for the future. Noah also had *conquering-faith*. Noah moved with fear because God warned him of future judgment. Noah conquered any fear by instant-obedience. Do you need *instant-faith*?

> *Lord, I want great faith. Give me insight-faith to know what You want me to do. Teach me to obey now—immediate-faith. Then give me conquering-faith to accomplish what You command. Then make me act quickly, instant-faith always looking for Your promise that will be fulfilled, i.e., future-faith. Isn't faith the evidence of things not seen, and the substance of things hoped for? Amen.*

What about the unsaved? Jesus said of Noah's generation, "They knew not until the flood came" (Matthew 24:34), then it was too late. It was not they did not know; Noah, a preacher of righteousness told them of a coming flood. The boat was also a warning. They heard and they saw, but they did not know, because they did not believe. Isn't that our job to tell them before it is too late?

Lord, You have great patience with people giving them time to hear and repent (2 Peter 3:9). Thank you for Your patience with me until I heard and believed. Now I will tell again my family and friends. Amen.

READING:

2 Peter 3:1-18

REFLECTION

_____

_____

_____

_____

_____

_____

_____

_____

_____

_____

_____

Day 33

ACTION-FAITH

"It was by faith that Noah built a large boat to save his family from the flood. He obeyed God, who warned him about things that had never happened before. By his faith Noah condemned the rest of the world, and he received the righteousness that comes by faith."

Hebrews 11:7, NLT

THE Bible commends Noah for his faith, "by faith Noah." Noah had a "stand-alone" faith that no one else on earth had. No one entered the ark with Noah, only his family. What did Noah's faith do, "prepared an ark" (v. 7)? Noah had *action-faith*, he didn't wait until it rained, nor did he wait for help from others. Noah's faith grabbed him and would not let go. It took 120 years to build the boat, and Noah kept building. There were no warning sprinkles of rain, only mist from the gourd to water everything (Genesis 2:5-6). There wasn't even a rainbow until after the flood.

Lord, give me action-faith like Noah so I will act on what You have said in Scriptures. Give me tenacity-faith to keep doing what You command in Your Word. Give me practical-faith to keep building and working when I don't see the end. Give me faith in You. Amen.

James tells us "faith without works is dead" (James 2:26). How do we know Noah had faith? He kept building the ark because God spoke to him. You cannot say you have faith if you don't have faith to study and know the Bible. If you don't have faith to worship Him! If you don't have faith to get your family and friends saved and secure in the ark, i.e., a picture of Christ who save us from the coming judgment of God.

Lord, I will declare my faith by studying Your Word and worshiping You daily and telling family and friends about salvation. I will declare my faith by obedience to Your Word and by seeking fellowship with You daily. Amen.

READING:

Genesis 7:1-23

REFLECTION

Day 34

DOOR IN THE BOAT

"Make a boat...put a door on the side."

Genesis 6:15-16, NLT

"I am the door. If anyone enters by Me,
he will be saved, and will go in and out and find pasture."

John 10:9, NKJV

COME thou and all thy house into the ark" (Genesis 7:1, KJV). God didn't say *go*...because God was in the boat. Noah had built it by faith with 120 years of hard labor, but God was in the boat. Does it make a difference to you where God is located? In the same way God invites, "come into My church...come into My salvation...come into My heaven." Would you mind being there if God was there? Would you want to go anywhere where God was not located? How safe was Noah and his family in the ark? As safe as the presence of God.

Jesus, You are the door to salvation. Because I believe in You, my sins are forgiven. Jesus, You are the door to heaven, I enter into You and I will go to heaven. I feel secure in Jesus and I love Him (John 14:20). Amen.

There are some who hope they will go to heaven when they die. They have doubts and hope to just get into heaven by the skin of their teeth. But Jesus is the door. When you enter Jesus, you get His life which is eternal life. When you are in Jesus you can have assurance for heaven. Eternal security is not in a place, it is in the Person of Jesus Christ. When Jesus lives in your heart you have all God gives to you.

Jesus, thank You for the door into the ark, it was the only way to get in. You are the only way to get into heaven. I believe in You and I will go through You—the door to heaven and eternal life. Amen.

READING:

Genesis 7:1-16, 8:1-22

REFLECTION

Day 35

INDIFFERENCE, IMMORALITY, IGNORANCE

"For as in the days before the flood, they were eating and drinking,
marrying and giving in marriage, until the day that Noah entered the ark,
and did not know until the flood came and took them all away,
so also will the coming of the Son of Man be."

Matthew 24:38-39

THREE words describe civilization in Noah's day. First was *indifference*. "They were eating... drinking...marrying." What does that mean? They were busy with their routine, thinking of material things and food, rather than God and spiritual things. Even Noah's preaching made no difference. The second word is *immorality*. We see in Genesis 6:1-8 that sex dominated their thinking, obviously all types of immorality. There were mixed marriages and intermarriages that God condemned (Genesis 6:1-18). Take time to listen to people around you talking. They talk about material possessions, and pleasures that they want. There is no thought of God, heaven, or of dying.

Lord, I see indifference everywhere. Make me sensitive to God and His plan for my life.
Help me look away from earthly possessions to see Jesus. I want to know Him, follow Him,
and be like Him. Amen.

The third word is *ignorance*. "They knew not until the flood came" (Matthew 24:24). They should have known because of Noah's preaching. The three-story boat should have warned them. They might tell God, "I didn't know," but Noah told them, but they did not listen, because they did not want to hear what he had to say. Will you listen when God speaks to you? How will you get your family and friends to listen to you about Jesus' return? You can pray! Make sure you live a good godly testimony before them.

Lord, I pray for family and friends who know of my salvation, but they don't join me. I pray for my testimony to the unsaved. May they hear and listen and turn to Jesus Christ. Use me as a witness. Amen.

READING:

2 Corinthians 5:14-21

REFLECTION

_____

_____

_____

_____

_____

_____

_____

_____

_____

_____

Day 36

FAITH PREPARES

"By faith Noah, being divinely warned of things not yet seen, moved with godly fear, prepared an ark for the saving of his household, by which he condemned the world and became heir of the righteousness which is according to faith."

Hebrews 11:7, NKJV

THE Bible said Noah "prepared an ark." What made him build a boat? He didn't wait till it started to rain; it would have been too late. When the Bible says, "by faith being warned of things not seen, moved with fear." His faith warned of the coming judgment. Here faith and foresight are linked together. When a person realizes they must die, and they realize the consequences of hell, their faith can save them. Many times, God uses fear and faith to save a lost person.

Lord, thank You for speaking to Noah to warn him of the coming judgment. Also, thank You for moving me to have faith in Jesus Christ for salvation. I trust You...love You...and want to serve You. Please use me for Your glory. Amen.

Jesus said, "But of that day and hour know no man...but only My Father" (Matthew 24:36). The unknown produces fear, whether it is an unknown disease, or an unknown bill, or any unknown thing that will hurt or kill. Let's get the message of Jesus Christ out to family and friends that Jesus can come at any time. Be ready! Also, we could die or be killed at any time. Let fear lead to faith in Jesus Christ.

Lord, thank You for giving saving-faith. I believe in Jesus! Now may I have faith like Noah, he built a boat to save himself and his family. Help my faith motivate me to ministry and action. Amen.

READING:

Matthew 24:27-44;

Hebrews 11:1-8

REFLECTION

Section 6

LOIS

A Grandmother Overcoming Obstacles

L OIS lived in the mountains in Lystra, off the beaten path. Only a few Jewish families lived in that isolated part of Asia Minor, today called Turkey. Lois married a Gentile, as did her daughter Eunice; probably because there were no Jewish boys available. There were not enough Jewish families to be large enough for a synagogue. So, with little godly influence, Lois the grandmother and Eunice the mother influenced Timothy to be a man of God.

Timothy became a Christian when Paul came to Lystra. Paul recognized the influence the two women had on Timothy when writing (2 Timothy 1:5, 3:14-15). Thus, a godly grandmother with little help or encouragement influenced her daughter to live for God, and then the two of them influenced Timothy.

Day 37

GRANDMOTHER LOIS

"When I call to remembrance the genuine faith that is in you,
which dwelt first in your grandmother Lois and your mother Eunice,
and I am persuaded is in you also."

2 Timothy 1:5

LOIS was born of Jewish parents. Growing up in Lystra, there were few Jewish boys to marry. The small town in the mountains had little commutation with the outside world. A visiting Rabbi was quoted, "Better marry a Gentile man and drag him into heaven than not marry at all." So, Lois influenced her children and grandchildren. Her daughter Eunice meaning "commended well" also married a Gentile. Then Timothy was born to Eunice, "his mother was a Jewish believer, but his father was a Greek" (Acts 16:1, NLT). God had a plan through two women isolated in a small town. Through them would come Timothy, an early Christian leader who influenced the future of Christianity.

Lord, thank You for my mother and father and thank You that I am born again. May I be
Your servant to influence many for You. Use me to reach beyond my family to influence Your
work around the world. Amen.

Because Lois and Eunice were dedicated Jewish women, they dedicated Timothy to the LORD God at an early age. Because of a Greek father, Timothy was not circumcised until Paul brought salvation to the family. "Timothy...circumcised" (Acts 16:3, NLT). Now, Timothy was ready to serve with Paul carrying the Gospel to the lost.

Lord, thank You for those who helped me find salvation and who taught me the Christian faith. Thank You for all in my home and church who influenced me to live for You. Amen.

READING:

Acts 16:1-10;

1 Timothy 1:18-19

REFLECTION

Day 38

TEACHING TIMOTHY

"These are the commands, decrees, and regulations that the Lord your
God commanded me to teach you. You must obey them in the land
you are about to enter and occupy, and you and your children
and grandchildren must fear the Lord your God as long as you live.
If you obey all his decrees and commands, you will enjoy a long life."

Deuteronomy 6:1-2, NLT

GRANDMOTHER Lois and mother Eunice took the commands in Deuteronomy seriously. It included, *grandmothers,* so Lois was involved in teaching young Timothy the Old Testament law, prophets and history. Did Eunice teach him the Psalms, Proverbs and the duties of a young Jewish boy to obey? Both are commended by Paul for teaching Timothy. "The genuine faith that is in you, which dwelt first in your grandmother Lois and your mother Eunice" (2 Timothy 1:5).

Lord, thank You for mothers and grandmothers who are faithful to You to teach their chil-
dren the Word of God. May my children and grandchildren be as well taught as Timothy.
Amen.

Lois and Eunice taught young Timothy to write and he began early copying the Scriptures as did all young Hebrew children in those days. But the Word of God was also written in Timothy's heart so he could preach where Paul sent him, and he could help Paul write his letters. The influence of a godly grandmother and mother goes much deeper than most realize. It lives beyond their lives in the children and grandchildren they teach and influence.

Lord, thank You for godly mothers and grandmothers. I ask that my daughters would be as godly as Lois and Eunice. Then I ask for them to be as influential in molding the lives of my grandchildren. Amen.

READING:

Deuteronomy 6:1-25

REFLECTION

Day 39

TEACH GENUINE FAITH

"When I call to remembrance the unfeigned faith that is in thee,
which dwelt first in thy grandmother Lois, and thy mother Eunice;
and I am persuaded that in thee also."

2 Timothy 1:5, KJV

LOIS had *unfeigned* faith. The word feigns describes an actor on a stage who wore a mask or played a role on stage. But Lois had unfeigned faith meaning she was not playing Christianity; she was not wearing a mask. It could be described as genuine faith. We know it was real faith because she poured it into young Timothy. Paul recognized its authenticity saying, "Continue in the things which you have learned and been assured" (2 Timothy 3:14). The greatest compliment to a teacher is the life of their students. The greatest compliment to a grandmother and mother is when their children and grandchildren live the faith, they taught them.

Lord, thank You for those who taught me faith in Jesus Christ. May I be as faithful to teach others as they were to teach me. Thank You for the influence of family in your church. May my faith continue Your influence in the church and around the world. Amen.

When Paul said *knowing whom*, the word is plural. Timothy was taught by both Eunice and Lois. They poured their character into Timothy, and we can see their influence in the continual ministry of Timothy in the pages of the New Testament.

Lord, thank You for faithful mothers and grandmothers who carry on Your ministry to influence their children and grandchildren. May I be faithful to all I have learned from many sources. Amen.

READING:

2 Timothy 1:1-18

REFLECTION

Day 40

EARLY INFLUENCES

"But you must remain faithful to the things you have been taught. You know
they are true, for you know you can trust those who taught you. You have been
taught the holy Scriptures from childhood, and they have given you the wisdom
to receive the salvation that comes by trusting in Christ Jesus."

2 Timothy 3:14-15, NLT

The word "childhood" *brethos* comes from breath, its first breathing as an embryo. Before Timothy could walk or talk, he was taught the Scriptures. Grandmother and mother probably said the Psalms to the baby before he could understand words. He probably learned to count numbers by the Ten Commandments. Both women told him stories—the great heroes and heroines of the faith from Scripture. The word for *Scripture* is graphee which meant *copied Scriptures*. Timothy learned to write copying the Word of God.

Lord, thank You for telling us to teach children the Word of God. I will obey and teach
them. Thank You for all those who taught me the Scriptures that changed my life. Amen.

Paul told Timothy to stay true to the faith. "Knowing from whom you learned them" (2 Timothy 3:14, KJV). The word *knowing* is not just acquired knowledge, but *oida* means innate knowledge. The grandmother and mother poured faith into Timothy so that it became part of his character growing up. Timothy became what the women taught him to be. That is the challenge for you to teach your children and grandchildren.

Lord, I pray for my children and grandchildren to be saved and to grow in Christ. May they grow up knowing all about Jesus and when they come of age, may they know Him as Savior and Lord. Amen.

READING:

2 Timothy 3:10-4:8

REFLECTION

Day 41

SALVATION

"Then came he to Derbe and Lystra: and, behold, a certain disciple
was there, named Timotheus, the son of a certain woman, which
was a Jewess, and believed; but his father was a Greek."

Acts 16:1, KJV

THERE were no synagogues in Lystra for Paul to attend, meaning there was not even 12 Jewish families. So, when Paul arrived in the city the second time, he gathered a few believers together. Eunice was among them, identified in the past tense as a believer. She was saved the first time Paul preached the Gospel there. In Second Timothy 1:5, it suggests Lois the grandmother was also was saved on that first trip to Lystra. They knew the Old Testament so when Paul told them the Messiah had to die for their sins and be raised again—they believed. When did you come to faith in Jesus? When was the first time you heard, or did it take a second time?

Lord, thank You for salvation. I know I am saved, and I pray to the Father that Jesus died
for my sins, and the Holy Spirit convicts me of my sins and brought me to salvation. Amen.

We don't know exactly when Timothy was saved, but it was under the influence of Paul. He wrote, "To Timothy, a true son in the faith" (1 Timothy 1:2). And again, Paul wrote, "To Timothy, my beloved son" (2 Timothy 1:2). His salvation comes from the godly influence of a grandmother and mother, mixed with the powerful influence of a man of God.

Lord, thank You for the influence of fathers, mothers, and grandparents in my life. Also,
thank You for the influence of Your servants both men and women who told me about sal-
vation...prayed for me...taught me... and encourage me to serve You. Amen.

READING:

1 Timothy 1:1-5;
2 Timothy 1:1-18

REFLECTION

_____
_____
_____
_____
_____
_____
_____
_____
_____
_____
_____
_____

Day 42

IN SPITE OF PERSECUTION

"Then some Jews arrived from Antioch and Iconium and won the crowds to their side. They stoned Paul and dragged him out of town, thinking he was dead. But as the believers gathered around him, he got up and went back into the town. The next day he left with Barnabas for Derbe."

Acts 14:19-20, NLT

TIMOTHY'S Christian faith was not shaken by Paul's stoning. We don't know if Timothy was in the crowd that gathered around Paul's body, and we don't know if Timothy prayed for Paul's healing. But we do know that Paul walked back to town, and the next day left for Derbe. We know God did a miracle in Paul's body. He immediately went back to ministry. "Persecution and afflictions" (2 Timothy 3:11) were witnessed by Timothy, it could be the young man's faith was strengthened by seeing Paul's experience and seeing Paul's miraculous recovery.

Lord, thank You for the life of Paul, especially for his endurance in spite of terrible persecution. May my faith be that strong if I have to suffer. Thank You for the life of Jesus Christ in me that gives me hope...and courage...and determination to serve. Amen.

Was Paul killed when stoned in Lystra? When Paul wrote 14 years later it pinpointed the time. "Such a one was caught up into the third heaven ...whether in the body or out of the body I do not know...he was caught up into Paradise" (2 Corinthians 12:1-4). Yes, it appears Paul died and was raised from the dead. Since Timothy was a witness to Paul's sufferings or death, this young man understood the sacrifice he would have to make in serving Christ. Are you willing to yield your life to Jesus Christ?

Lord, when I think of Christian martyrs, giving their life for You, I realize You gave me a good life. May I use my testimony to glorify You. Use my life for Your purpose—by life or death. Amen.

READING:

Acts 14:1-28;

2 Corinthians 12:1-10

REFLECTION

Day 43

THROUGH MANY LIMITATIONS

"I remember your genuine faith, for you share the faith that first
filled your grandmother Lois and your mother, Eunice.
And I know that same faith continues strong in you."

2 Timothy 1:5, NLT

A grandmother or mother may have many limitations, but they can still have a life-changing influence on their children. The women did not have a male role model to influence Timothy. They didn't have a fulltime minister to teach, fellowship, or support. They were stuck up in the mountains off the beaten path of civilization. They had little outside help, but they had incredible inner strength. They had the Word of God, and they had the working of God Almighty in their life. With only their faith and inner assurance they poured their strength into Timothy, and God used him to influence the cause of Christ.

Lord, when I complain that I don't have much, remind me of Your powerful influence
through Lois and Eunice. I give you my weakness and doubts. Empty me of self-pity and
complaints. Give me spiritual eyes to see Your vision for my life. Then give me strength to
do it. Amen.

We see the great attention to small details in the education of Timothy. Even the use of the Greek word, *graphee* for Scriptures, suggests they were guiding Timothy as he copied the Scriptures. Did he copy the Scriptures that became his own personal Bible? Probably! Did he memorize great passages of Scriptures? Probably! Did it influence Timothy's life? Absolutely!

Lord, I will give attention to reading the whole Bible and at the same time give attention to the small details in Scriptures. Speak to me with great lessons to learn, will I also give attention to the small details of the faith. Amen.

READING:

2 Timothy 3:10-16;

Joshua 1:2-9

REFLECTION

Section 7

PAUL

A Spiritual Disciple-Making Grandfather

THIS section is not about the fourth generation, i.e. great-grandparents. No! That is a wonderful topic, and if grandparents would be all God wants of them, they will see their children, the fourth generation serving Jesus Christ.

This section is about the first generation, it is about you becoming a "great" grandparent. It is about becoming better than you expect, or even better than you have talents to become. The word "great" is in quotation marks to make it stand apart, like you a grandparent can stand apart. The word *great* suggest you can become greater than your talents, and greater than expected.

But remember it is Christ who makes you "great," so this section focuses on seven principles to make any grandparent a "great" grandparent.

Day 44	First Be a Disciple
Day 45	Disciple-Making Grandparents
Day 46	Grandparents Pour Out Their Souls
Day 47	Total Discipleship Dedicated to Be Like Jesus
Day 48	A Disciple Follows Jesus
Day 49	Discipleship by Example
Day 50	Disciple-Making by Instruction

Day 44

FIRST BE A DISCIPLE

"Then he said to the crowd, 'If any of you wants to be my follower,
you must give up your own way, take up your cross daily,
and follow me. If you try to hang on to your life, you will lose it.
But if you give up your life for my sake, you will save it.'"

Luke 9:23-24, NLT

TO be a disciple-maker, you must first become a disciple. Paul was a disciple/apostle, yet not one of the original 12 called by Jesus to follow Him and learn from Him. One of the criteria to be an apostle was to have seen Jesus in His resurrected body (Acts 1:20-22). Paul testified Jesus "was seen by...all the apostles. Last of all...I saw him" (1 Corinthians 15:7-8). An apostle must learn from Jesus (Paul learned in Arabia, Galatians 1:17). Then a disciple must be commissioned and sent into ministry (Galatians 1:15-16). Therefore, Paul the disciple-maker could challenge Timothy, "And the things that thou hast heard of me...commit thou to faithful men" (2 Timothy 2:2, KJV).

Lord, Paul saw Jesus and shared that experience with Timothy and others. I have seen Jesus in Scriptures and I experience Him living in my heart. Help me be a disciple-maker so that others will tell what God has done in their hearts. Amen.

Another criteria of a disciple is one who "takes up Jesus' cross and daily follows Him" (Luke 9:23, ELT). Paul certainty took up the cross for he suffered continually for the Gospel ministry (2 Corinthians 4:8-18, 6:4-10). Paul was a true disciple who followed Jesus and he gave his life to make disciples out of Timothy and all others he led to saving knowledge of Jesus Christ. Therefore, before you can become a disciple-maker, you must first be a disciple and demonstrate the mark of a disciple of Jesus Christ.

Lord, thank You for the example of Paul's discipleship. I want to have the ministry and influence of Paul. I will be crucified with Christ (Galatians 2:20), and I will live like Jesus and become like Jesus (Philippians 3:10-14). Help me learn...grow...minister...and pray like Paul. Amen.

READING:

Luke 9:18-26;

2 Corinthians 4:5-18, 6:1-10

REFLECTION

_____

_____

_____

_____

_____

_____

_____

_____

_____

_____

_____

Day 45

DISCIPLE-MAKING
GRANDPARENTS

"And the things that thou hast heard of me among many witnesses, the same commit thou to faithful men, who shall be able to teach others also."

2 Timothy 2:2, KJV

FOUR generations are the acid test of reproducing yourself into another person. In today's verse, Paul the first generation was the spiritual father to Timothy. Paul expected Timothy to live and minister the way he did. Second-generation Timothy poured himself into the third-generation "faithful men." The strength that Timothy received from Paul was passed to the third generation. But we don't know that faithful men really got the life that Paul passed to Timothy until they can pass it on to the fourth generation of "others." Each generation must faithfully pass on everything they received to the generation that follows them.

Lord, thank You for those who led me to Jesus Christ. Also thank You for those who taught me the Bible and Christian living and how to serve You. Help me grow to become as strong as those who taught me. Help me pass all those lessons on to another. Amen.

It all depends on the first generation—the grandparents—who they are and how they lived. They must pass it to the next generation. Oh, that grandparent was stronger, so each succeeding generation would be stronger. Grandparents are not really reproducing—reproducers until their grandchildren live, believe, and love the Lord the way they originally did.

Lord, thank You for my children, may they be as strong in Christ as I am. Thank You for my grandchildren, may they learn from both their parents and me, a grandparent, and live like us or better. Amen.

READING:

2 Timothy 2:1-26

REFLECTION

_____

_____

_____

_____

_____

_____

_____

_____

_____

_____

Day 46

GRANDPARENTS POUR OUT THEIR SOULS

"But we were as gentle among you as a mother feeding and caring for her own children. We loved you dearly—so dearly that we gave you not only God's message, but our own lives too."

1 Thessalonians 2:7-8, TLB

PAUL motivated Timothy to be a reproducer by pouring his own soul and passion into him. It wasn't just teaching doctrine, it wasn't just learning Bible facts, and it wasn't just learning methods of ministry. Paul poured his own passion for Jesus Christ into Timothy. Paul did such a thorough job that Timothy did the same to those he taught. Timothy became a reproducer of himself into the third generation. That is the standard for all believers today. Each must pour himself/ herself into another disciple, so the next generation is as strong as the first, so they do it to the fourth generation.

Lord, thank You for those who were responsible for my salvation. May I pour their passion into those I lead to Christ. I want the passion of those who led me to Christ to pass through me to more people. Amen.

Being a grandparent is not just reproducing a physical child. It means more. You want your children to love Jesus Christ as much as you do, so they can pour that passion into your grandchildren. Then you pray that both your children and grandchildren will love Jesus more than you ever did. You want them to serve in ministry more than you ever did.

Lord, I pray for my children to love You as much as I do. If they don't, forgive me where I failed. Give me another chance with my grandchildren and I will pour my faith and love into them. Lord may my faith continue in my children and grandchildren. Amen.

READING:

1 Thessalonians 2:1-19

REFLECTION

Day 47

TOTAL DISCIPLESHIP

Dedicated to be Like Jesus

"For God called you to do good, even if it means suffering, just as Christ suffered for you. He is your example, and you must follow in his steps."

1 Peter 2:21, NLT

TO be a disciple-maker like Paul, you must first become a disciple like Paul, or, the above Scripture refer to Peter, also a disciple. The challenge is to live like Jesus, to minister like Jesus, and to follow His steps. But before you can do anything for Jesus you must become like Jesus. But we are all sinners, how can we live like Jesus and minister like Him. The answer—we can't. But in salvation Jesus indwells us to give us eternal life and transform us. That happens as we yield to Christ...learn Christ...ask Christ to use us...and let Christ's power become our power in ministry. We must learn to allow Jesus Christ in us—flow through us to others.

Lord, that is a big challenge. "Self" gets in the way, so I yield myself to You. Come minister through me and help me and use me to carry out Your will. Before I become a disciple-maker, I must first become Your disciple. Make it happen in me. Amen.

Learn the first steps in becoming a disciple from Jesus who said, "If anyone desires to come after Me, let him deny himself" (Luke 9:23). That is a hard lesson to learn, but it begins, "Not I but Christ" (Galatians 2:20). This is part of the process of "crucifying self" so Jesus Christ can be seen in us. Then His power works through us. When we become that kind of disciple, then we are ready to become a disciple-maker. In this series it means you are spiritual grandparent.

Lord, I want to learn the first hard lesson, help me deny self. It's hard to do, but I pray with Paul, "I can do all things through Christ who strengthens me" (Philippians 1:21). I want to follow You, and learn You, and become like You. Lord make me Your disciple, then I can be a disciple-maker. Amen.

READING:

1 Peter 2:21-25;

Philippians 2:20-21;

2 Corinthians 12:1-15

REFLECTION

Day 48

A DISCIPLE FOLLOWS JESUS

*"If you abide in My word, you are My disciples indeed. And you
shall know the truth, and the truth shall make you free."*

John 8:31-32, NKJV

A disciple obeys and lives the Word of God. Jesus referred to the Word of God in two ways. First the word spoken by Jesus is the living Word of God. Second, the Bible written is the inspired Word of God. But in both cases, Jesus' Words must enter into the man/woman of God, control his/her life and the power and message of Jesus must flow into their life to transform them. It is not about how the disciples learn; it is about Jesus changing their life. It is not eloquent words, or the method used to teach/preach the Bible, it is about Jesus. When you become a disciple of Jesus, you follow a Person—you follow Jesus Christ.

Lord, I want to be Your disciple. I will learn Your Word, and let it control my life. I will memorize and meditate on Your Word, and let its message be the theme of my ministry to others. I will let the Christ of the Bible be my testimony and I will share Him with others. Amen.

There are many ways to learn the Bible. You can read it...memorize it...and mediate on it. But the best way to learn the Bible is to share it with others. You pour into their lives what God has used to fill your life and transform you. Many learning techniques are great but when your heart is hungry for Jesus let the Word of God fill you (Jeremiah 15:16). Let its strength fill you and let its transforming power work in your heart.

Lord, I want to be Your devoted disciple, so I will dedicate myself to learning the Bible thoroughly and completely. I will immerse myself in Scriptures and let its life-changing power transform me. Amen.

READING:

Psalm 119:9-16; 105-112;
John 8:1-12, 30-36

REFLECTION

_____

_____

_____

_____

_____

_____

_____

_____

_____

_____

_____

Day 49

DISCIPLESHIP BY EXAMPLE

*"But you, Timothy, certainly know what I teach, and how I live, and what
my purpose in life is. You know my faith, my patience, my love, and my
endurance. You know how much persecution and suffering I have endured.
You know all about how I was persecuted in Antioch, Iconium, and
Lystra—but the Lord rescued me from all of it."*

2 Timothy 3:10-11, NLT

AS a disciple, Paul was a compelling example. But he was also a disciple-maker by example. Notice what examples Paul holds up to Timothy. First, Paul held the *correct doctrine*, that is the foundation. Next is *manner of life* that also is the basis for asking anyone to follow you, as you follow Jesus. The third was *long-suffering*. Here Paul reminds Timothy of harsh travels, and suffering from weather conditions and self-discipline to endure them all. The fourth is *love and perseverance* that involves giving yourself to those you love. Isn't that a definition of love? As Albert Schweitzer observed, "Example is not the main thing, it is the only thing."

Lord, thank You for the example of Paul who was faithful in all the above areas. I want to live and minster like Paul. Use me to teach Your Word. Help me be an example in faithfulness, love, and perseverance. Amen.

Paul's fifth example was *persecution*. He included Lystra where Paul was stoned. Some say he died, but God raised him up to continue his ministry. What a great example to young Timothy in his teens who witnessed Paul's willingness to die and suffer for the Gospel. This event may be the crowing influence of Paul's life and ministry to young Timothy.

Lord, I have taken up Your cross to follow You. I don't think about martyrdom, but I am willing to give my life for You because You gave Your life for me. I will serve You as long as I live, and when I die, I will come home to live with You. Amen.

READING:

Acts 14:6-22;

2 Corinthians 12:1-12;

2 Timothy 3:10-17

REFLECTION

DISCIPLE-MAKING BY INSTRUCTION

"And the things that you have heard from me among many witnesses, commit these to faithful men who will be able to teach others also."

2 Timothy 2:2, NKJV

HOW did Paul disciple young Timothy? Through many ways. First Timothy heard many sermons from Paul, probably the essence of all the New Testament books Paul wrote came from his preaching. Next, there were private conversations, sometimes solving problems in a church, where Timothy learned churchmanship. But some conversations were structural. Paul explained how churches should be organized, administered, and minister. This is included in "you heard from me" (v. 2). Some of these great lessons can be taught in a few seconds, because the learner is both needy and willing to learn. Then other discussions take a long time to explain, some Paul had to repeat the lessons many times. Perhaps the lesson of predestination, or God's eternal plan with Jews, or those involving the nature and attributes of God.

Lord, help me learn as much about You as I possibly can know. I want to serve You success-fully, so help me learn what to do, and how to do it. I want to pass on to others what I have learned. Again, give me grace and wisdom to be a disciple-maker. Amen.

Paul's was an encourager. He was not reluctant to build up young Timothy and motivate him to be faithful in his personal life, and faithful in service. What Paul told Timothy, he expected to be passed on to the third generation. What grandparents tell their children; they expect the message to be passed on to their grandchildren. "Stir up" (2 Timothy 1:6). "Be strong" (2 Timothy 2:1). "Neglect not" (1 Timothy 4:4). "Continue" (2 Timothy 3:14).

Lord, I want to be as faithful to You as those who taught me to live for You. But Lord, I want to go farther in my faith, and I want to do more than them. I am not in completion; I just want to do as much as possible while I am here. Amen.

READING:

2 Timothy 4:1-11

REFLECTION

PART THREE

GRANDPARENTS IN THE BIBLE

LESSONS

INTRODUCTION

A. LESSONS IN THIS SERIES

1. Jacob – a spiritual giver.

2. Naomi – a compromising grandmother becomes godly example.

3. Asa – a revival grandson came from an ungodly grandmother.

4. Noah – a stumbling block.

5. Lois – a grandmother overcoming obstacles.

6. Paul – a spiritual disciple-making grandfather.

B. INTRODUCTION

1. The **4/14 window**. Most receive Christ between the ages of 4 and 14.

2. There are **50 percent** more grandparents today than in 1950.

3. Most become a grandparent at age **47**. The youngest grandparent-generation ever.

4. Today's children are a **lost generation**, who are the rebellious baby boomers, also called a loss generation.

5. Two myths about grandparenting:

   a. The grandparent's main task is to **enjoy grandchildren** (no heritage builders).

   b. Grandparenting is a **leisure life** (no disciplining).

6. According to a survey, very few grandparents feel they are influential.

7. The main task for each generation:

Father/husband	The head (<u>leader</u>) of the family
Mother/wife	The <u>helpmeet</u>
Children	Learn and obey
Grandparent	**<u>Heritage</u>**

8. 35% American children live in a single parent home. They need grandparents. Some states have <u>**50%**</u>.

9. 10% of American children are being raised by **<u>grandparents</u>**.

10. A larger percentage of grandparents move in with their children to raise **<u>grandchildren</u>**.

11. Grandparents grieve the loss of their **<u>children's marriage</u>**.

12. Most grandparents are as **<u>clueless</u>** about how to influence their grandchildren for God as they were with their own children.

C. FOUR THINGS GRANDPARENTS SHOULD DO

1. **<u>Bless</u>** their grandchildren. More than money, things, or food, give them spiritual security, a significant purpose in life, and sufficient resources.

2. Leave a **<u>legacy</u>**. When they get the phone call, "Gramps died" what will they remember most about you, and miss the most?

3. Carry the torch, **<u>pass it on</u>**. The Gospel is the torch, don't drop it, hide it, and don't change it.

4. Communicate a standard of **<u>moral living</u>** in an immoral world. Be their spiritual GPS **<u>Gramps</u>**.

D. TEN POINTS OF LIGHT FOR GRANDPARENTS

1. Grandparents can best show a **vision of the future**. They view the future through the lenses of past failures and successes.

2. Grandparents are effective because they get a **second chance**.

3. They set a moral example for children and grandchildren. "Life is tough, but it is tougher when you are stupid" —**John Wayne**

4. Grandparents are more like **God** than when they were parents. As parents, produced community, **set rules**, enforced rules, **punished**, rewarded. As grandparents: they listen, give good things, fellowship, are patient, **show grace**, overlook faults, etc. God doesn't **mock**, put down, or criticize.

5. The joy of grandparenting is blessing them, "**add value**."

6. Grandparents **communicate** the values and attitudes of tradition by example, gifts, actions, and love. **Heritage makers** in lives.

7. How they feel about their grandchildren is how grandchildren will **feel about themselves**.

8. God has a **plan** for each grandchild; it is the responsibility of grandparents to help them find it.

9. Grandparents **can** be the kindest, most patient generation. But a few decide to be **crotchety**.

10. Grandparents can be a ***Bridge Over Troubled Water***:

> *When you're weary, feeling small,*
> *When tears are in your eyes, I will dry them all.*
> *I'm on your side, when times get tough,*
> *And friends just can't be found,*
> *Like a bridge over troubled waters*
> *I will lay me down.*
> *When you're down and out,*
> *When you're on the street,*
> *When evening falls so hard,*
> *I will comfort you,*
> *I will take your hand*
> *When darkness comes,*
> *And pain is all around*
> *Like a bridge over troubled waters*
> *I will lay me down.*
>
> —Simon and Garfunkel

Lesson 1:
QUESTIONS

INTRODUCTION

A. LESSONS IN THIS SERIES

1. Jacob – a spiritual giver.

2. Naomi – a compromising grandmother becomes godly example.

3. Asa – a revival grandson came from an ungodly grandmother.

4. Noah – a stumbling block.

5. Lois – a grandmother overcoming obstacles.

6. Paul – a spiritual disciple-making grandfather.

B. INTRODUCTION

1. The _____ . Most receive Christ between the ages of 4 and 14.

2. There are _____ more grandparents today than in 1950.

3. Most become a grandparent at age _____ . The youngest grandparent-generation ever.

4. Today's children are a _____ , who are the rebellious baby boomers, also called a loss generation.

5. Two myths about grandparenting:

   c. The grandparent's main task is to _____ (no heritage builders).

d. Grandparenting is a _____ (no disciplining).

6. According to a survey, very few grandparents feel they are influential.

7. The main task for each generation:

   Father/husband   The head (_____) of the family

   Mother/wife   The _____

   Children   Learn and obey

   Grandparent   _____

8. 35% American children live in a single parent home. They need grandparents. Some states have _____ .

9. 10% of American children are being raised by _____ .

10. A larger percentage of grandparents move in with their children to raise _____ .

11. Grandparents grieve the loss of their _____ .

12. Most grandparents are as _____ about how to influence their grandchildren for God as they were with their own children.

C. FOUR THINGS GRANDPARENTS SHOULD DO

1. _____ their grandchildren. More than money, things, or food, give them spiritual security, a significant purpose in life, and sufficient resources.

2. Leave a _____ . When they get the phone call, "Gramps died" what will they remember most about you, and miss the most?

3. Carry the torch, _____ . The Gospel is the torch, don't drop it, hide it, and don't change it.

4. Communicate a standard of _____ in an immoral world. Be their spiritual GPS _____ .

D. TEN POINTS OF LIGHT FOR GRANDPARENTS

1. Grandparents can best show a _____ . They view the future through the lenses of past failures and successes.

2. Grandparents are effective because they get a _____ .

3. They set a moral example for children and grandchildren. "Life is tough, but it is tougher when you are stupid" — _____

4. Grandparents are more like _____ than when they were parents. As parents, produced community, _____ , enforced rules, _____ , rewarded. As grandparents: they listen, give good things, fellowship, are patient, _____ , overlook faults, etc. God doesn't _____ , put down, or criticize.

5. The joy of grandparenting is blessing them, " _____ ."

6. Grandparents _____ the values and attitudes of tradition by example, gifts, actions, and love. _____ in lives.

7. How they feel about their grandchildren is how grandchildren will _____ .

8. God has a _____ for each grandchild; it is the responsibility of grandparents to help them find it.

9. Grandparents _____ be the kindest, most patient generation. But a few decide to be _____ .

10. Grandparents can be a _____ :

When you're weary, feeling small,
When tears are in your eyes, I will dry them all.
I'm on your side, when times get tough,
And friends just can't be found,
Like a bridge over troubled waters
I will lay me down.
When you're down and out,
When you're on the street,
When evening falls so hard,
I will comfort you,
I will take your hand
When darkness comes,
And pain is all around
Like a bridge over troubled waters
I will lay me down.

—Simon and Garfunkel

JACOB

The Spiritual Giver

A. INTRODUCTION: GENESIS 48:1-22

1. What can a "**poor**" grandfather give to a son who has everything?

2. What can an **absentee** grandfather give to children he seldom sees?

3. What can a **physically weak** grandfather give to his grandchildren?

4. What can a grandfather give, who has **nothing left** to give?

B. FOUR THINGS GRANDFATHER SAID TO THEM

1. Jacob told them **his testimony**. "God Almighty appeared to me at Luz in the land of Canaan" (v. 3). Was this Jacob's salvation experience? "The angel which redeemed me from evil" (v. 16).

WHAT'S INVOLVED IN A TESTIMONY?

What you **were like** before salvation.

What you did to **receive Christ**.

How you were **changed**.

"God before whom my fathers, Abraham, and Isaac did walk, the God which fed me all my life long until this day" (v. 15).

2. Jacob told them the **Word of God**. He told them God's **name**, God's **words**, and God's **expectations** (vv. 15-17).

3. Jacob told them the four-fold promise of God (v. 4).

   a. **Wealth**. "Behold I will make thee fruitful."

   b. **Influence**. "I will multiply thee."

   c. **Nation**. "I will make of thee a multitude of people."

   d. **Land**. "I will give this land to thy seed after thee for an everlasting possession."

OMITTED FROM ABRAHAM'S COVENANT

1. Bless these who bless you.

2. Curse your enemies.

3. Make name great.

4. Jacob told them about their **grandmother**. "When I came from Padan, Rachel died by me in the land of Canaan in the way, when yet there was a little way to come to Ephrath, and I buried her there" (v. 7).

   a. Your grandmother died in **travel**.

   b. I **was there** when she died.

   c. We were **almost home**.

   d. She was buried by the **road**.

C. FOUR THINGS GRANDFATHER DID FOR THEM

1. Jacob **adopted** them. "Now these two sons, Ephraim and Manasseh...are mine" (v. 5). The boys were half Hebrew and half Egyptian.

2. Jacob **kissed and hugged** them. Jacob showed his affection. "He kissed them and embraced them" (v. 10).

3. Jacob laid **his hands on them**. "And Israel stretched out his right hand, and laid it upon Ephraim's head, who was the younger, and his left hand upon Manasseh's head, guiding his hands wittingly; for Manasseh was the firstborn" (v. 14). The word *wittingly* means Jacob knew what he was doing.

4. Jacob **blessed** his grandchildren. "By faith Jacob when he was dying, blessed both the sons of Joseph" (Heb. 11:21).

HOW TO BLESS CHILDREN

Step 1: A meaningful touch.

Step 2: Blessing with a spoken word.

Step 3: Attach high value to the one being blessed.

Step 4: Picture a special future for the one being blessed.

Step 5: An active commitment to fulfilling the blessing.

From *God Bless You*, by Elmer Towns

D. FOUR THINGS GRANDFATHER GAVE THEM

1. Jacob gave them **his name**. Jacob adopted the two boys. "They are mine" (v. 5). "Let my name be upon them, and the name of my father Abraham and Isaac" (v. 16).

2. Jacob gave **God's future** to them. "Let them grow into a multitude in the midst of the earth" (v. 16). "And he blessed them that day, saying, in thee shall Israel bless, saying, God make thee as Ephraim and as Manasseh; and he set Ephraim before Manasseh" (v. 20).

3. Jacob gave them **his love**.

4. Jacob gave them an **example of worship**.
   a. The **position** of worship. "He (Jacob) bowed himself with his face to the earth" (v. 12).
   b. The **attitude** of worship. "Jacob...worshipped, leaning upon the top of his staff" (Heb. 11:21).

E. FOUR LESSONS TO TAKE AWAY

1. Grandparents should be concerned about the **spiritual condition** of their grandchildren.

2. Grandparents shall be a **spiritual example**.

3. Grandparents should give their **testimony**.

4. Grandparents should bless **naturally** and spiritually.

Lesson 2:

JACOB

The Spiritual Giver

A. INTRODUCTION: GENESIS 48:1-22

1. What can a " _____ " grandfather give to a son who has everything?

2. What can an _____ grandfather give to children he seldom sees?

3. What can a _____ grandfather give to his grandchildren?

4. What can a grandfather give, who has _____ to give?

B. FOUR THINGS GRANDFATHER SAID TO THEM

1. Jacob told them _____ . "God Almighty appeared to me at Luz in the land of Canaan" (v. 3). Was this Jacob's salvation experience? "The angel which redeemed me from evil" (v. 16).

WHAT'S INVOLVED IN A TESTIMONY?

What you _____ before salvation.

What you did to _____ .

How you were _____ .

"God before whom my fathers, Abraham, and Isaac did walk, the God which fed me all my life long until this day" (v. 15).

2. Jacob told them the _____ . He told them God's _____ , God's
   _____ , and God's _____ (vv. 15-17).

3. Jacob told them the four-fold promise of God (v. 4).

   a. _____ . "Behold I will make thee fruitful."

   b. _____ . "I will multiply thee."

   c. _____ . "I will make of thee a multitude of people."

   d. _____ . "I will give this land to thy seed after thee for an everlasting possession."

OMITTED FROM ABRAHAM'S COVENANT

1. Bless these who bless you.

2. Curse your enemies.

3. Make name great.

4. Jacob told them about their _____ . "When I came from Padan, Rachel died by me in the land of Canaan in the way, when yet there was a little way to come to Ephrath, and I buried her there" (v. 7).

   a. Your grandmother died in _____ .

   b. I _____ when she died.

   c. We were _____ .

   d. She was buried by the _____ .

C. FOUR THINGS GRANDFATHER DID FOR THEM

1. Jacob _____ them. "Now these two sons, Ephraim and Manasseh...are mine" (v. 5). The boys were half Hebrew and half Egyptian.

2. Jacob _____ them. Jacob showed his affection. "He kissed them and embraced them" (v. 10).

3. Jacob laid _____ . "And Israel stretched out his right hand, and laid it upon Ephraim's head, who was the younger, and his left hand upon Manasseh's head, guiding his hands wittingly; for Manasseh was the firstborn" (v. 14). The word *wittingly* means Jacob knew what he was doing.

4. Jacob _____ his grandchildren. "By faith Jacob when he was dying, blessed both the sons of Joseph" (Heb. 11:21).

HOW TO BLESS CHILDREN

Step 1: A meaningful touch.

Step 2: Blessing with a spoken word.

Step 3: Attach high value to the one being blessed.

Step 4: Picture a special future for the one being blessed.

Step 5: An active commitment to fulfilling the blessing.

From *God Bless You*, by Elmer Towns

D. FOUR THINGS GRANDFATHER GAVE THEM

1. Jacob gave them _____ . Jacob adopted the two boys. "They are mine" (v. 5). "Let my name be upon them, and the name of my father Abraham and Isaac" (v. 16).

2. Jacob gave _____ to them. "Let them grow into a multitude in the midst of the earth" (v. 16). "And he blessed them that day, saying, in thee shall Israel bless, saying, God make thee as Ephraim and as Manasseh; and he set Ephraim before Manasseh" (v. 20).

3. Jacob gave them _____ .

4. Jacob gave them an _____ .

   a. The _____ of worship. "He (Jacob) bowed himself with his face to the earth" (v. 12).

   b. The _____ of worship. "Jacob...worshipped, leaning upon the top of his staff" (Heb. 11:21).

E. FOUR LESSONS TO TAKE AWAY

1. Grandparents should be concerned about the _____ of their grandchildren.

2. Grandparents shall be a _____ .

3. Grandparents should give their _____ .

4. Grandparents should bless _____ and spiritually.

Lesson 3:

NAOMI

A Compromising Mother Becomes a Godly Grandmother

A. HOW NAOMI COMPROMISED

1. She compromised her **spiritual priorities**.

    a. Did not continue in difficulties. "A famine in the land" (Ruth 1:1).

    b. Enticed by the well-watered plains of Moab (1:1).

    c. Left the Promised Land. "Ephrathites of Bethlehem, Judah" (1:2).

2. She compromised her commitment **to the Lord**. When Ruth, her daughter-in-law wanted to go with Naomi, she directed her to go back to her foreign god. "Look, your sister-in-law has gone back to her people and to her gods; return after your sister-in-law" (1:15).

3. Naomi compromised her **family influence**. Naomi's son, Chilion, married outside the faith (1:4).

4. Naomi **criticized** God's provision for her. "I went out full, and the Lord has brought me home again empty" (1:21).

B. NAOMI'S REPENTANCE SEEN IN HER ACTIONS

1. **Naomi recognized God's punishment.** Naomi recognized God's punishment. "The Lord hath caused me to suffer, and the Almighty has sent me such tragedy" (1:21, NLB).

---

2. **Naomi's counsel toward family heritage**. When Ruth "happened" on Boaz's field, Naomi said, "Blessed be he of the Lord, who has not forsaken His kindness to the living and the dead! And Naomi said to her, this man is a relation of ours, one of our close relatives" (2:20).

3. Naomi counseled toward **redemption**. "Then Naomi her mother-in- law said unto her, 'My daughter, shall I not seek security for you, that it may be well with you?'" (3:1).

4. Naomi counseled **patience and trust**. "Then she (Naomi) said, 'Sit still, my daughter...for the man will not rest until he has concluded the matter this day'" (3:18).

C. THE BLESSING ON GRANDMOTHER NAOMI

"Then the women said to Naomi, 'Blessed be the Lord, who has not left you this day without a close relative; and may his name be famous in Israel! And may he be to you a restorer of life and a nourisher of your old age; for your daughter-in-law, who loves you, who is better to you than seven sons, has borne him'" (Ruth 4:14-15).

1. Naomi is given **more importance** in the Bible than Ruth.

    a. The women blessed Naomi (4:14).

    b. The child is recognized as "kin" to Naomi (4:14).

    c. Naomi had oversight for the child's care (4:16).

2. The child is **identified** with this grandmother (not father or grandfather). Note: legal line not through Naomi and Elimelech (4:21).

3. The child Obed would be **famous in Israel**.

    a. The word famous means, "name is proclaimed widely."

    b. Obed was the **great grandfather** of Daniel.

    c. Obed comes from two words, (1) Obadiah i.e., a **worshipper of God**, (2) *ebed*, i.e., **servant**. Obed was a true servant and worshipper of the Lord.

4. The child gave Grandmother Naomi a **purpose in life**.

   a. Naomi had been a **compromiser**, but she became a woman of **conviction**.

   b. Naomi didn't have **any hope**. She told Ruth, "Turn back, my daughters, go-for I am too old to have a husband. If I should say I have hope, if I should have a husband tonight and should also bear sons" (1:12). But God gave her a **new life**. "He (Obed) shall be unto thee, a restorer of life" (4:15).

   c. Naomi had no **spiritual energy**. "Call me Mara, for the Almighty hath dealt very bitterly with me" (1:20). But Obed **nourished** her old age. "And may he (Obed) be to you a restorer of life and a nourisher of your old age" (4:15).

5. Naomi gained **the love** of her daughter-in-law. "Then the women said to Naomi, 'Blessed be the Lord... your daughter-in-law, who loves you, who is better to you than seven sons." (4:14-15).

6. Naomi had the responsibility of **influencing** the child.

   a. Naomi was given a **second chance** to rear a son.

   b. A rich man like Boaz would have **a maid** for children, i.e., he got Naomi.

   c. "Then Naomi took the child and laid him on her bosom, and became a nurse to him" (4:16).

Lesson 3:
QUESTIONS

NAOMI

A Compromising Mother Becomes a Godly Grandmother

A. HOW NAOMI COMPROMISED

1. She compromised her _____ .

    a. Did not continue in difficulties. "A famine in the land" (Ruth 1:1).

    b. Enticed by the well-watered plains of Moab (1:1).

    c. Left the Promised Land. "Ephrathites of Bethlehem, Judah" (1:2).

2. She compromised her commitment _____ . When Ruth, her daughter-in-law wanted to go with Naomi, she directed her to go back to her foreign god. "Look, your sister-in-law has gone back to her people and to her gods; return after your sister-in-law" (1:15).

3. Naomi compromised her _____ . Naomi's son, Chilion, married outside the faith (1:4).

4. Naomi _____ God's provision for her. "I went out full, and the Lord has brought me home again empty" (1:21).

B. NAOMI'S REPENTANCE SEEN IN HER ACTIONS

1. _____ . Naomi recognized God's punishment. "The Lord hath caused me to suffer, and the Almighty has sent me such tragedy" (1:21, NLB).

2. _____ . When Ruth "happened" on Boaz's field, Naomi said, "Blessed be he of the Lord, who has not forsaken His kindness to the living and the dead! And Naomi said to her, this man is a relation of ours, one of our close relatives" (2:20).

3. Naomi counseled toward _____ . "Then Naomi her mother-in-law said unto her, 'My daughter, shall I not seek security for you, that it may be well with you?'" (3:1).

4. Naomi counseled _____ . "Then she (Naomi) said, 'Sit still, my daughter...for the man will not rest until he has concluded the matter this day'" (3:18).

C. THE BLESSING ON GRANDMOTHER NAOMI

"Then the women said to Naomi, 'Blessed be the Lord, who has not left you this day without a close relative; and may his name be famous in Israel! And may he be to you a restorer of life and a nourisher of your old age; for your daughter-in-law, who loves you, who is better to you than seven sons, has borne him'" (Ruth 4:14-15).

1. Naomi is given _____ in the Bible than Ruth.

    a. The women blessed Naomi (4:14).

    b. The child is recognized as "kin" to Naomi (4:14).

    c. Naomi had oversight for the child's care (4:16).

2. The child is _____ with this grandmother (not father or grandfather). Note: legal line not through Naomi and Elimelech (4:21).

3. The child Obed would be _____ .

    a. The word famous means, "name is proclaimed widely."

    b. Obed was the _____ of Daniel.

    c. Obed comes from two words, (1) Obadiah i.e., a _____ , (2) *ebed*, i.e., _____ . Obed was a true servant and worshipper of the Lord.

4. The child gave Grandmother Naomi a _____ .

    a. Naomi had been a _____ , but she became a woman of _____ .

    b. Naomi didn't have _____ . She told Ruth, "Turn back, my daughters, go-for I am too old to have a husband. If I should say I have hope, if I should have a husband tonight and should also bear sons" (1:12). But God gave her a _____ . "He (Obed) shall be unto thee, a restorer of life" (4:15).

    c. Naomi had no _____ . "Call me Mara, for the Almighty hath dealt very bitterly with me" (1:20). But Obed _____ her old age. "And may he (Obed) be to you a restorer of life and a nourisher of your old age" (4:15).

5. Naomi gained _____ of her daughter-in-law. "Then the women said to Naomi, 'Blessed be the Lord...your daughter-in-law, who loves you, who is better to you than seven sons." (4:14-15).

6. Naomi had the responsibility of _____ the child.

    a. Naomi was given a _____ to rear a son.

    b. A rich man like Boaz would have _____ for children, i.e., he got Naomi.

    c. "Then Naomi took the child and laid him on her bosom, and became a nurse to him" (4:16).

ASA

A Revival Grandson Came From an Ungodly Grandmother

"In the twentieth year of Jeroboam king of Israel, Asa became king over Judah. And he reigned forty-one years in Jerusalem. His grandmother's name was Maachah the granddaughter of Absalom. Asa did what was right in the eyes of the Lord, as did his father David. And he banished the perverted persons from the land, and removed all the idols that his fathers had made. Also, he removed Maachah his grandmother from being queen mother, because she had made an obscene image of Asherah. And Asa cut down her obscene image and burned it by the brook Kidron" (I Kings 15:9-13).

A. MAACHAH: AN UNGODLY GRANDMOTHER

1. **Fighter**. Her name Maachah means "fighting" or "oppression."

2. **Rebellious**. Maachah was rebellious like her grandfather Absalom. "His (Abijam) mother's name was Maachah, the daughter of Absalom (Absalom)" (1 Kings 15:2).

   a. Absalom **murdered** his brother Amnon. "Absalom had commanded...when I say strike Amnon, then kill him" (2 Sam. 13:28).

   b. Absalom pretended to be loyal to his father David. "So, Absalom stole the hearts of the men of Israel" (2 Sam. 15:6).

   c. Absalom tried to **kill** his father David. "Make haste to depart from the city of David lest he overtake us suddenly...and strike the city with the edge of the sword" (2 Sam. 15:14).

3. Grandmother Maachah influenced her husband Rehoboam to **compromise**.

   a. "Rehoboam loved Maachah the daughter of Absalom more than all his wives and his concubines... and Rehoboam made Abijah the son of Maachah as chief to be leader over his brethren, for he intended to make him King" (2 Chron. 11:20-22).

   b. Rehoboam's sin **split** the kingdom.

   c. Rehoboam's continuing sin **corrupted** the kingdom. "And he (Rehoboam) did evil because he did not prepare his heart to seek the Lord" (2 Chron. 12:14).

4. Grandmother Maachah gave her son an **evil name**. The son of Maachah was Abijah (2 Chron. 12:16 ff) whose name means, "The Lord is my Father," but the boy also was given the name Abijam, which means "My father is Yam" a Canaanite god of the sea.

5. Maachah supported sexual **sodomy**. "And Asa took away all the sodomites out of the land, and removed all the (filthy) idols that his father (Abijam) had made" (1 Kings 15:12).

6. Maachah worshipped **false gods**. "Asa removed all the idols that his father and mother had made" (1 Kings 15:12-13, ELT).

7. Maachah secretly had a **sexual** goddess-idol. She had made an obscene image to Asherah. "And Asa cut down her obscene idol and burned it by the brook Kidron" (1 Kings 15:13).

    a. Idols usually represent a **spirit-demon**.

    b. Maachah was utterly **evil**.

B. ASA, A GODLY GRANDSON

1. Asa reacted to the **sins** of his father. "Abijam walked in all the sins of his father which he had done before him (evil example), and his heart was not perfect with the Lord his God, or the heart of David" (1 Kings 15:3-4). The principle: extreme abuses lead to reformation.

2. God **sovereignly prepared** Asa to carry on the godly rule of David. "Nevertheless, for David's sake did the Lord his God give him a lamp in Jerusalem to set up his son (Asa) after him, and to establish Jerusalem" (1 Kings 15:4).

3. Asa began with reforms (2 Chronicles 14:2-7).

    a. Repented of **outward idolatry**. "He (Asa) removed the altars of the foreign gods and the high places and broke down the sacred pillars and cut down the wooden images" (2 Chron. 14:3).

    b. Commanded the people to serve **the Lord**. "He (Asa) commanded Judah to seek the Lord God of their fathers and to do the law and the commandment" (2 Chron. 14:4).

    c. Asa **armed and fortified** the nation. "He (Asa) built fortified cities in Judah, for the land had rest; he had no war in those years" (2 Chron. 14:6). "And Asa had an army of three hundred thousand from Judah ...and from Benjamin two hundred and eighty thousand men" (2 Chron. 14:8).

    d. Asa relied on the Lord to **defend the nation**. When attacked, "Asa cried out to the Lord his God, and said, 'Lord, it is nothing for You to help, whether with many or with those who have no power; help us, O Lord our God, for we rest on You, and in Your name we go against this multitude. O Lord, You are our God; do not let man prevail against You!'" (2 Chron. 14:11).

4. Asa led the nation in revival (2 Chronicles 15:1-19).

   a. Had the people **taught the Scriptures**. "For a long time Israel has been without the true God, without teaching priest, without law" (2 Chron. 15:3).

   b. Reinstituted **blood sacrifice**. "Restored the altar of the Lord that was before the vestibule of the Lord" (2 Chron. 15:8).

   c. Celebrated the **feast to the Lord**. "They gathered together at Jerusalem...and they offered to the Lord" (2 Chron. 15:10-11).

   d. Led the people in **dedication**. "They entered into the covenant to seek the Lord God of their fathers with all their heart and with all their soul" (2 Chron. 15:12).

   e. Actually, took **an oath**. "Then they took an oath before the Lord with a loud voice, with shouting, and trumpets, and ram's horn" (2 Chron. 15:14).

C. LESSONS TO TAKE AWAY

1. Sometimes the sinful excesses in parents and grandparents produce an **opposite reaction** in children. Notice the conditions when Asa was a child. "There was no peace to the one who went out...but great turmoil...nation was destroyed by nation, and city by city" (2 Chron. 15:5-6).

2. Sometimes the evil influence of parents produces children **more evil** than themselves, i.e., Maachah was more evil than Absalom.

3. Be sure your sin will **expose you**. Maachah's sin was known and dealt with.

4. Cursed to the **third or fourth generation**. God had promised, "The Lord thy God is a jealous God, visiting the iniquity of the fathers upon the children to the third and fourth generation of them that hate me" (Ex. 20:5). Absalom → Maachah → Abijam → Asa

5. God **sovereignly** raises up righteous children.

6. Sometimes a grandchild has to **deal with the sins** of a grandparent.

7. A grandchild can become more godly as he/she grows older, i.e., Asa began with **reforms**, but eventually brought in a **revival**.

Lesson 4:

ASA

A Revival Grandson Came From an Ungodly Grandmother

"In the twentieth year of Jeroboam king of Israel, Asa became king over Judah. And he reigned forty-one years in Jerusalem. His grandmother's name was Maachah the granddaughter of Absalom. Asa did what was right in the eyes of the Lord, as did his father David. And he banished the perverted persons from the land, and removed all the idols that his fathers had made. Also, he removed Maachah his grandmother from being queen mother, because she had made an obscene image of Asherah. And Asa cut down her obscene image and burned it by the brook Kidron" (I Kings 15:9-13).

A. MAACHAH: AN UNGODLY GRANDMOTHER

1. _____ . Her name Maachah means "fighting" or "oppression."

2. _____ . Maachah was rebellious like her grandfather Absalom. "His (Abijam) mother's name was Maachah, the daughter of Absalom (Absalom)" (1 Kings 15:2).

   a. Absalom _____ his brother Amnon. "Absalom had commanded...when I say strike Amnon, then kill him" (2 Sam. 13:28).

   b. Absalom pretended to be loyal to his father David. "So, Absalom stole the hearts of the men of Israel" (2 Sam. 15:6).

   c. Absalom tried to _____ his father David. "Make haste to depart from the city of David lest he overtake us suddenly...and strike the city with the edge of the sword" (2 Sam. 15:14).

3. Grandmother Maachah influenced her husband Rehoboam to _____ .

   a. "Rehoboam loved Maachah the daughter of Absalom more than all his wives and his concubines... and Rehoboam made Abijah the son of Maachah as chief to be leader over his brethren, for he intended to make him King" (2 Chron. 11:20-22).

   b. Rehoboam's sin _____ the kingdom.

   c. Rehoboam's continuing sin _____ the kingdom. "And he (Rehoboam) did evil because he did not prepare his heart to seek the Lord" (2 Chron. 12:14).

4. Grandmother Maachah gave her son an _____ . The son of Maachah was Abijah (2 Chron. 12:16 ff) whose name means, "The Lord is my Father," but the boy also was given the name Abijam, which means "My father is Yam" a Canaanite god of the sea.

5. Maachah supported sexual _____ . "And Asa took away all the sodomites out of the land, and removed all the (filthy) idols that his father (Abijam) had made" (1 Kings 15:12).

6. Maachah worshipped _____ . "Asa removed all the idols that his father and mother had made" (1 Kings 15:12-13, ELT).

7. Maachah secretly had a _____ goddess-idol. She had made an obscene image to Asherah. "And Asa cut down her obscene idol and burned it by the brook Kidron" (1 Kings 15:13).

   a. Idols usually represent a _____ .

   b. Maachah was utterly _____ .

B. ASA, A GODLY GRANDSON

1. Asa reacted to the _____ of his father. "Abijam walked in all the sins of his father which he had done before him (evil example), and his heart was not perfect with the Lord his God, or the heart of David" (1 Kings 15:3-4). The principle: extreme abuses lead to reformation.

2. God _____ Asa to carry on the godly rule of David. "Nevertheless, for David's sake did the Lord his God give him a lamp in Jerusalem to set up his son (Asa) after him, and to establish Jerusalem" (1 Kings 15:4).

3. Asa began with reforms (2 Chronicles 14:2-7).

   a. Repented of _____ . "He (Asa) removed the altars of the foreign gods and the high places and broke down the sacred pillars and cut down the wooden images" (2 Chron. 14:3).

   b. Commanded the people to serve _____ . "He (Asa) commanded Judah to seek the Lord God of their fathers and to do the law and the commandment" (2 Chron. 14:4).

   c. Asa _____ the nation. "He (Asa) built fortified cities in Judah, for the land had rest; he had no war in those years" (2 Chron. 14:6). "And Asa had an army of three hundred thousand from Judah ...and from Benjamin two hundred and eighty thousand men" (2 Chron. 14:8).

   d. Asa relied on the Lord to _____ . When attacked, "Asa cried out to the Lord his God, and said, 'Lord, it is nothing for You to help, whether with many or with those who have no power; help us, O Lord our God, for we rest on You, and in Your name we go against this multitude. O Lord, You are our God; do not let man prevail against You!'" (2 Chron. 14:11).

4. Asa led the nation in revival (2 Chronicles 15:1-19).

   a. Had the people _____ . "For a long time Israel has been without the true God, without teaching priest, without law" (2 Chron. 15:3).

   b. Reinstituted _____ . "Restored the altar of the Lord that was before the vestibule of the Lord" (2 Chron. 15:8).

   c. Celebrated the _____ . "They gathered together at Jerusalem...and they offered to the Lord" (2 Chron. 15:10-11).

   d. Led the people in _____ . "They entered into the covenant to seek the Lord God of their fathers with all their heart and with all their soul" (2 Chron. 15:12).

   e. Actually, took _____ . "Then they took an oath before the Lord with a loud voice, with shouting, and trumpets, and ram's horn" (2 Chron. 15:14).

C. LESSONS TO TAKE AWAY

1. Sometimes the sinful excesses in parents and grandparents produce an _____ in children. Notice the conditions when Asa was a child. "There was no peace to the one who went out... but great turmoil...nation was destroyed by nation, and city by city" (2 Chron. 15:5-6).

2. Sometimes the evil influence of parents produces children _____ than themselves, i.e., Maachah was more evil than Absalom.

3. Be sure your sin will _____ . Maachah's sin was known and dealt with.

4. Cursed to the _____ . God had promised, "The Lord thy God is a jealous God, visiting the iniquity of the fathers upon the children to the third and fourth generation of them that hate me" (Ex. 20:5). Absalom → Maachah → Abijam → Asa

5. God _____ raises up righteous children.

6. Sometimes a grandchild has to _____ of a grandparent.

7. A grandchild can become more godly as he/she grows older, i.e., Asa began with _____ , but eventually brought in a _____ .

NOAH

A. WHAT WE KNOW FOR SURE

Grandfather – Noah –<u>Sinned</u>

Father – Ham – Gossiped

Grandson – Canaan – <u>Laughed</u>

"And Noah began to be a farmer, and he planted a vineyard. Then he drank of the wine and was drunk, and became uncovered in his tent. And Ham, the father of Canaan, saw the nakedness of his father, and told his two brothers outside. But Shem and Japheth took a garment, laid it on both their shoulders, and went backward and covered the nakedness of their father. Their faces were turned away, and they did not see their father's nakedness. So, Noah awoke from his wine, and knew what his younger son had done to him. Then he said: 'Cursed be Canaan; a servant of servants He shall be to his brethren'" (Gen. 9:20-25).

1. <u>Godly</u>. What is known about Noah? "Noah was a just man and perfect...and Noah walked with God" (Gen. 6:9).

2. <u>Warned of judgment</u>. Why did Noah build an ark? "By faith Noah being divinely warned of things not yet seen moved with godly fear, prepared an ark...by which he condemned the world" (Heb. 11:7).

3. <u>Carpenter</u>. What was Noah's occupation? "God said to Noah...make yourself an ark of gopher wood" (Gen. 6:14).

4. <u>Preacher</u>. How did Noah warn the world? "Noah...a preacher of righteousness" (2 Peter 2:5).

5. <u>Drinking</u>. What sins did Jesus mention Noah preached against?" As the days of Noah were, so also will be the coming of the Son of Man...drinking...until the day Noah entered the ark" (Matt. 24:37-38).

6. <u>Satan worship</u>. What were other sins the people committed? (Gen. 6:1-13).

7. <u>God called</u>. When did Noah enter the ark? "The Lord said to Noah, 'Come thou and all thy house into the ark'" (Gen. 7:1). He was 601 years old (Gen. 8:13, NLT).

8. <u>A farmer</u>. What was Noah's new occupation after the flood? "Noah began to be a husbandman, and planted a vineyard" (9:20).

9. What was Noah's threefold sin? "He (Noah) drank of the wine, and was drunken, and he was uncovered within the tent" (Gen. 9:21).

   a. <u>Drunken</u>. He preached against it.

   b. <u>Exposure</u>. He uncovered himself, i.e., *gulah* (reflective).

   c. <u>Lack of role model</u>.

10. How did Noah know? "Noah awoke from his wine, and knew what his younger son had done to him" (9:24).

   a. Special <u>revelation</u>.

   b. <u>Inquiry</u>. He asked or was told.

   c. <u>Memory</u>. A drunk man remembers some things.

B. WHAT WAS THE SIN OF HAM AND CANAAN?

1. <u>Seeing only</u>. "Ham, the father of Canaan saw the nakedness of his father, and told his two brethren" (Gen. 9:22). What went with seeing?

   a. <u>Lust</u>.

   b. <u>Mockery.</u>

   c. <u>Rejection</u> of father's authority to His God. (Morris)

   d. <u>Not covering</u>, i.e., showing disrespect.

2. <u>Not seeing</u>. "Shem and Japheth took a garment, and laid it upon their shoulders, and went backward, and covered the nakedness of their father;.... and saw not their father's nakedness" (Gen. 9:23).

3. Why curse Canaan?

   a. **Youngest**. Ham was the youngest son of Noah, and Canaan youngest son of Ham (Gen. 10:6).

   b. **Divine curse**. This was not an "angry" grandfather. Since only God could know the future, Noah spoke by God's revelation. God cursed Canaan for what he did, and what He was to become.

   c. Noah recognized a **rebellious attitude and perverse lust**. Noah/God saw a weakness in Canaan and knew it would be perpetuated.

   d. **Third generation** always suffers the most, "cursed be Canaan, a servant of servants, shall he be to his brethren" (Gen. 9:25).

4. When was the curse carried out?

   a. The Canaanites become a **lustful people**. God describes them "uncovered the nakedness" (Lev. 18:3 ff).

   b. The curse was carried out when Joshua and Israel **conquered** the Canaanites (Joshua 11:12).

C. WHAT LESSONS CAN BE LEARNED ABOUT SINNING GRANDPARENTS

1. You never get **too old to quit sinning**.

2. You can fall at your **greatest strength**. "Let him that thinketh he standeth take heed lest he fall" (1 Cor. 10:12, KJV).

3. Your fall can hurt **your family**. "Cursed be Canaan."

4. Your fall can come after God has **greatly used you**. Noah, Elijah, Peter, Paul, Uriah, David.

5. Just because you have done a lot for God, doesn't mean He will **overlook your sin in old age**.

6. The careless root of sin in a grandfather or father (lust or rebellion) can have **disastrous results** in grandchildren.

7. Drunkenness is not a **private sin**, nor is it something God overlooks.

8. The body is the temple of the Holy Spirit, and the child of God should be modest.

   a. Applies to **all ages**.

   b. Applies to **sexual exposure**.

   c. Applies to **sexual viewing, i.e., lust**.

9. Hitherto repressed **lust and sexual fantasies** will surface when given the opportunity.

D. WHAT GRANDPARENTS AND GRANDCHILDREN NEED TO KNOW

1. God **provides victory**. "No temptation has overtaken you except such as is common to man; but God is faithful, who will not allow you to be tempted beyond what you are able, but with the temptation will also make the way of escape, that you may be able to bear it" (1 Cor. 10:13).

2. God **lives in your body**. "He who commits sexual immorality, sins against his own body. Do you not know that your body is the temple of the Holy Spirit, who is in you...you are not your own" (1 Cor. 6:18-19).

3. Old age sin **will disqualify you**. "But I discipline my body and bring it into subjection, lest, when I have preached to others, I myself should become disqualified" (1 Cor. 9:27).

Lesson 5:

NOAH

A. WHAT WE KNOW FOR SURE

Grandfather – Noah – _____

Father – Ham – Gossiped

Grandson – Canaan – _____

"And Noah began to be a farmer, and he planted a vineyard. Then he drank of the wine and was drunk, and became uncovered in his tent. And Ham, the father of Canaan, saw the nakedness of his father, and told his two brothers outside. But Shem and Japheth took a garment, laid it on both their shoulders, and went backward and covered the nakedness of their father. Their faces were turned away, and they did not see their father's nakedness. So, Noah awoke from his wine, and knew what his younger son had done to him. Then he said: 'Cursed be Canaan; a servant of servants He shall be to his brethren'" (Gen. 9:20-25).

1. _____ . What is known about Noah? "Noah was a just man and perfect...and Noah walked with God" (Gen. 6:9).

2. _____ . Why did Noah build an ark? "By faith Noah being divinely warned of things not yet seen moved with godly fear, prepared an ark...by which he condemned the world" (Heb. 11:7).

3. _____ . What was Noah's occupation? "God said to Noah...make yourself an ark of gopher wood" (Gen. 6:14).

4. _____ . How did Noah warn the world? "Noah...a preacher of righteousness" (2 Peter 2:5).

5. _____ . What sins did Jesus mention Noah preached against?" As the days of Noah were, so also will be the coming of the Son of Man...drinking...until the day Noah entered the ark" (Matt. 24:37-38).

6. _____ . What were other sins the people committed? (Gen. 6:1-13).

7. _____ . When did Noah enter the ark? "The Lord said to Noah, 'Come thou and all thy house into the ark'" (Gen. 7:1). He was 601 years old (Gen. 8:13, NLT).

8. _____ . What was Noah's new occupation after the flood? "Noah began to be a husbandman, and planted a vineyard" (9:20).

9. What was Noah's threefold sin? "He (Noah) drank of the wine, and was drunken, and he was uncovered within the tent" (Gen. 9:21).

   a. _____ . He preached against it.

   b. _____ . He uncovered himself, i.e., *gulah* (reflective).

   c. _____ .

10. How did Noah know? "Noah awoke from his wine, and knew what his younger son had done to him" (9:24).

   a. Special _____ .

   b. _____ . He asked or was told.

   c. _____ . A drunk man remembers some things.

B. WHAT WAS THE SIN OF HAM AND CANAAN?

1. _____ . "Ham, the father of Canaan saw the nakedness of his father, and told his two brethren" (Gen. 9:22). What went with seeing?

   a. _____ .

   b. _____ .

   c. _____ of father's authority to His God. (Morris)

   d. _____ , i.e., showing disrespect.

2. _____ . "Shem and Japheth took a garment, and laid it upon their shoulders, and went backward, and covered the nakedness of their father;.... and saw not their father's nakedness" (Gen. 9:23).

3. Why curse Canaan?

   a. _____ . Ham was the youngest son of Noah, and Canaan youngest son of Ham (Gen. 10:6).

   b. _____ . This was not an "angry" grandfather. Since only God could know the future, Noah spoke by God's revelation. God cursed Canaan for what he did, and what He was to become.

   c. Noah recognized a _____ . Noah/God saw a weakness in Canaan and knew it would be perpetuated.

   d. _____ always suffers the most, "cursed be Canaan, a servant of servants, shall he be to his brethren" (Gen. 9:25).

4. When was the curse carried out?

   a. The Canaanites become a _____ . God describes them "uncovered the nakedness" (Lev. 18:3 ff).

   b. The curse was carried out when Joshua and Israel _____ the Canaanites (Joshua 11:12).

C. WHAT LESSONS CAN BE LEARNED ABOUT SINNING GRANDPARENTS

1. You never get _____ .

2. You can fall at your _____ . "Let him that thinketh he standeth take heed lest he fall" (1 Cor. 10:12, KJV).

3. Your fall can hurt _____ . "Cursed be Canaan."

4. Your fall can come after God has _____ . Noah, Elijah, Peter, Paul, Uriah, David.

5. Just because you have done a lot for God, doesn't mean He will _____ .

6. The careless root of sin in a grandfather or father (lust or rebellion) can have _____ in grandchildren.

7. Drunkenness is not a _____ , nor is it something God overlooks.

8. The body is the temple of the Holy Spirit, and the child of God should be modest.

   a. Applies to _____ .

   b. Applies to _____ .

   c. Applies to _____ .

9. Hitherto repressed _____ will surface when given the opportunity.

D. WHAT GRANDPARENTS AND GRANDCHILDREN NEED TO KNOW

1. God _____ . "No temptation has overtaken you except such as is common to man; but God is faithful, who will not allow you to be tempted beyond what you are able, but with the temptation will also make the way of escape, that you may be able to bear it" (1 Cor. 10:13).

2. God _____ . "He who commits sexual immorality, sins against his own body. Do you not know that your body is the temple of the Holy Spirit, who is in you…you are not your own" (1 Cor. 6:18-19).

3. Old age sin _____ . "But I discipline my body and bring it into subjection, lest, when I have preached to others, I myself should become disqualified" (1 Cor. 9:27).

Lesson 6:

LOIS

A Grandmother Overcoming Obstacles

A. LOIS: LIVING BEYOND HER CIRCUMSTANCES

1. Married a **Gentile** just as her daughter Eunice. "Timothy, the son of a certain Jewish woman (Eunice) who believed, but his father was a Greek" (Acts 16:1).

2. What was her life in Lystra?

   a. Not enough Jewish families for a **synagogue**.

   b. Not any **civilized** advantage.

   c. Not many **Roman** citizens.

3. Lois expected a son but got a **daughter**. "Thy grandmother Lois, and thy mother Eunice" (2 Tim. 1:3).

4. Lois became a **genuine** believer. Paul said, "I call to remembrance the unfeigned faith that is in you (Timothy), which dwelt first in your grandmother Lois" (2 Tim. 1:5). Unfeigned means genuine, not a play actor repeating lines.

5. Lois and Eunice **poured their faith** into Timothy. "Continue in the things which you (Timothy) have been assured, knowing for whom you have learned them" (2 Tim. 3:14).

   a. The word "whom" is plural, **both taught**.

   b. The word "knowing" is *oida*, i.e., innate knowledge. Their teaching becomes more than knowledge, it became **his conviction**.

   c. The word "continue" means the women laid a **foundation** on which Paul and Timothy built.

6. Lois and Eunice began **teaching early**. "That from childhood you have known the Holy Scriptures, which are able to make you wise for salvation" (2 Tim. 3:15).

226 GRANDPARENTS IN THE BIBLE

a. The word "childhood" is *brephos*, which means embryo or newborn baby.

b. The word "known" is *oida*, i.e., innate knowledge.

c. Holy Scriptures is *graphe*, i.e., writings, which is plural **all parts** of the Word of God.

d. "Make you wise into" Greek suggests "motion into." The women were **moving** Timothy into salvation.

7. The women prepared the **spiritual foundation** for Timothy's conversion. "When I (Paul), call to remembrance the unfeigned faith that is in you, which dwelt first in your grandmother Lois and your mother Eunice, and I am persuaded is in you also" (2 Tim. 1:5).

B. PAUL BUILT ON LOIS AND EUNICE

1. The women **were converted** on Paul's first trip. (Acts 14:6-23). Paul returned on his second trip. "Then he came to Derbe and Lystra, and behold a certain disciple was there, named Timothy, the son of a certain Jewish woman who believed, but his father was a Greek" (Acts 16:1). "Believed" is past tense.

2. Timothy **believed in Christ** under Paul's ministry. "To Timothy, my true son in the faith" (1 Tim. 1:2). "To Timothy my beloved son" (2 Tim. 1:2).

3. Timothy believed **in spite of persecution**. "The Jews ...stoned Paul and dragged him out of the city (Lystra) supposing him to be dead" (Acts 14:19). Timothy was probably an eyewitness. "You have fully known my doctrine, manner of life...persecutions, afflictions, which came upon me at Antioch, at Iconium, at Lystra" (2 Tim. 3:10-11).

4. Timothy was **recommended** by the church leaders at Lystra. "Do not neglect the gift that is in you... with the laying on of hands of the presbytery" (1 Tim. 4:14). They would have endorsed the training given by Lois and Eunice.

5. Timothy was **ordained** by Paul. "Stir up the gift of God which is in you through the laying on of my hands" (2 Tim. 1:6).

C. LESSONS TO TAKE AWAY

1. When a grandmother has many limitations, she can be a great influence for God **through your children**.

2. Godly children are not automatically raised. It takes:

    a. **Early** instruction

    b. **Plain** instruction

    c. **Frequent** instruction

    d. **Patient** instruction

    (Adapted from John Wesley)

3. Your home can be a great godly influence, even when a church is not **available to help**.

4. Every grandmother should get the help of a **godly role model** to influence her grandchildren.

5. Giving attention to **small details** in a child's education will influence his/her total life.

6. When grandparents can't be all they want to be in life, at least they can be faithful in what's **given them in life**.

Lesson 6:

QUESTIONS

LOIS

A Grandmother Overcoming Obstacles

A. LOIS: LIVING BEYOND HER CIRCUMSTANCES

1. Married a _____ just as her daughter Eunice. "Timothy, the son of a certain Jewish woman (Eunice) who believed, but his father was a Greek" (Acts 16:1).

2. What was her life in Lystra?

   a. Not enough Jewish families for a _____ .

   b. Not any _____ advantage.

   c. Not many _____ citizens.

3. Lois expected a son but got a _____ . "Thy grandmother Lois, and thy mother Eunice" (2 Tim. 1:3).

4. Lois became a _____ believer. Paul said, "I call to remembrance the unfeigned faith that is in you (Timothy), which dwelt first in your grandmother Lois" (2 Tim. 1:5). Unfeigned means genuine, not a play actor repeating lines.

5. Lois and Eunice _____ into Timothy. "Continue in the things which you (Timothy) have been assured, knowing for whom you have learned them" (2 Tim. 3:14).

   a. The word "whom" is plural, _____ .

   b. The word "knowing" is *oida*, i.e., innate knowledge. Their teaching becomes more than knowledge, it became _____ .

   c. The word "continue" means the women laid a _____ on which Paul and Timothy built.

6. Lois and Eunice began _____ . "That from childhood you have known the Holy Scriptures, which are able to make you wise for salvation" (2 Tim. 3:15).

   a. The word "childhood" is *brephos*, which means embryo or newborn baby.

   b. The word "known" is *oida*, i.e., innate knowledge.

   c. Holy Scriptures is *graphe*, i.e., writings, which is plural _____ of the Word of God.

   d. "Make you wise into" Greek suggests "motion into." The women were _____ Timothy into salvation.

7. The women prepared the _____ for Timothy's conversion. "When I (Paul), call to remembrance the unfeigned faith that is in you, which dwelt first in your grandmother Lois and your mother Eunice, and I am persuaded is in you also" (2 Tim. 1:5).

B. PAUL BUILT ON LOIS AND EUNICE

1. The women _____ on Paul's first trip. (Acts 14:6-23). Paul returned on his second trip. "Then he came to Derbe and Lystra, and behold a certain disciple was there, named Timothy, the son of a certain Jewish woman who believed, but his father was a Greek" (Acts 16:1). "Believed" is past tense.

2. Timothy _____ under Paul's ministry. "To Timothy, my true son in the faith" (1 Tim. 1:2). "To Timothy my beloved son" (2 Tim. 1:2).

3. Timothy believed _____ . "The Jews...stoned Paul and dragged him out of the city (Lystra) supposing him to be dead" (Acts 14:19). Timothy was probably an eyewitness. "You have fully known my doctrine, manner of life...persecutions, afflictions, which came upon me at Antioch, at Iconium, at Lystra" (2 Tim. 3:10-11).

4. Timothy was _____ by the church leaders at Lystra. "Do not neglect the gift that is in you...with the laying on of hands of the presbytery" (1 Tim. 4:14). They would have endorsed the training given by Lois and Eunice.

5. Timothy was _____ by Paul. "Stir up the gift of God which is in you through the laying on of my hands" (2 Tim. 1:6).

C. LESSONS TO TAKE AWAY

1. When a grandmother has many limitations, she can be a great influence for God
   _____ .

2. Godly children are not automatically raised. It takes:

   a. _____ instruction

   b. _____ instruction

   c. _____ instruction

   d. _____ instruction

   (Adapted from John Wesley)

3. Your home can be a great godly influence, even when a church is not _____ .

4. Every grandmother should get the help of a _____ to influence her grandchildren.

5. Giving attention to _____ in a child's education will influence his/her total life.

6. When grandparents can't be all they want to be in life, at least they can be faithful in what's
   _____ .

PAUL

A Spiritual Disciple-Making Grandfather

"And the things that you have heard from me among many witnesses, commit these to faithful men who will be able to teach others also"

(2 Timothy 2:2).

Spiritual Grandfather – Paul – **Disciple-maker**

Son in ministry – Timothy – **Learner**

Third Generation – Faithful men – **Passed lessons on**

Fourth Generation – Others – **The proof of Christianity**

A. WHAT GRANDPARENTS DO THAT PARENTS DON'T DO

1. Grandparents make you feel **grown up**, while parents treat you as a **child**.

2. Grandparents can deal with **positive gentleness**, while parents must deal with **negative consequences**.

3. Grandparents point out your **future greatness**, while parents must deal with your **present shortcomings**.

4. Grandparents can **build individual initiative**, while parents must deal with your personal **responsibility and accountability**.

5. Grandparents have learned what is **eternally important**, and can overlook **immediate issues**.

B. WHAT IS A DISCIPLE-MAKING GRANDPARENT?

1. 1. You are a reproducer of <u>reproducers</u>.

   a. Because children are <u>mimickers,</u> they <u>live out</u> your examples.

   b. How you <u>influence them</u> is how they will be grandparents for future generations.

      <u>Paul</u>

         <u>Timothy</u>

            <u>Faithful men</u>

               <u>Others</u>

2. Your life will outlive your <u>lessons</u>.

3. You pour <u>your soul</u> into them. "As apostles of Christ...we were gentle among you as a parent cherishing a baby...giving you not only the gospel, but we poured our own lives into you" (1 Thess. 2:7-8, ELT).

4. You become <u>necessary</u> to them.

5. You have not finished until they pour <u>into others</u>, what you poured into them.

C. WHAT DOES A DISCIPLE LOOK LIKE?

1. Makes a <u>radical decision</u> for salvation. "Then He said to them all, 'If anyone desires to come after Me, let him deny himself, and take up his cross daily, and follow Me'" (Luke 9:23).

2. Has a dedication to be <u>like Jesus</u>. "Christ...leaving us an example that we should follow His steps" (1 Peter 2:21).

3. Learns to <u>abide</u> in Christ. "I am the Vine; you are the branches. He who abides in Me, and I in him, bears much fruit; for without Me you can do nothing" (John 15:5).

4. Learns to live by the <u>Scriptures</u>. "If you abide in My Word, you are My disciples indeed. And you shall know the truth, and the truth will make you free" (John 8:31-32).

5. Knows how to <u>pray</u>. "If you abide in Me, and My words abide in you, you will ask what you desire, and it shall be done for you" (John 15:7).

6. Makes <u>love the distinguishing mark of life</u>. "A new commandment I give to you, that you love one another; as I have loved you, that you also love one another" (John 13:34).

7. Testifies to and serves **others**. "Greater love has no one than this, than to lay down one's life for his friends" (John 15:13).

D. HOW DISCIPLE-MAKERS DO IT

1. By **example**. Paul told Timothy, "You have carefully followed My doctrine, manner of life, purpose, faith, longsuffering, love, perseverance, persecution..." (2 Tim. 3:10-11).

    "Example is not the main thing; it is the only thing"

    —Albert Schweitzer

2. By **association**. Paul called Timothy, "My beloved son" (2 Tim. 1:2).

3. By **assignment**. Paul sent Timothy to minister in Corinth, Macedonia, Philippi, Thessalonica, etc.

4. By **instruction**. Timothy heard Paul preach publicly and privately, i.e., "heard of me."

5. By **private counsel**. The two personal letters are reflections of their private conversations.

6. By **promotion**. Paul listed Timothy's name with his six times. Paul publicly expressed appreciation for Timothy (1 Cor. 4:17), and told the Philippians, "For I have no one like-minded (like Timothy) who will care for your state" (Phil. 2:20).

7. By **prodding**. Timothy needed a "jump start." "Stir up the gift of God which is in you" (2 Tim. 1:6). "Be strong" (2 Tim. 2:1).

PAUL

A Spiritual Disciple-Making Grandfather

*"And the things that you have heard from me among many witnesses, commit
these to faithful men who will be able to teach others also"*

(2 Timothy 2:2).

Spiritual Grandfather – Paul – _____

Son in ministry – Timothy – _____

Third Generation – Faithful men – _____

Fourth Generation – Others – _____

A. WHAT GRANDPARENTS DO THAT PARENTS DON'T DO

1. Grandparents make you feel _____ , while parents treat you as a _____ .

2. Grandparents can deal with _____ , while parents must deal with
   _____ .

3. Grandparents point out your _____ _____ , while parents must deal
   with your _____ .

4. Grandparents can _____ , while parents must deal with your
   personal _____ .

5. Grandparents have learned what is _____ , and can overlook
   _____ .

B. WHAT IS A DISCIPLE-MAKING GRANDPARENT?

1. 1. You are a reproducer of _____ .

   a. Because children are _____ , they _____ your examples.

   b. How you _____ is how they will be grandparents for future
      generations.

      _____

         _____

            _____

               _____

2. Your life will outlive your _____ .

3. You pour _____ into them. "As apostles of Christ...we were gentle among you as a
   parent cherishing a baby...giving you not only the gospel, but we poured our own lives into you"
   (1 Thess. 2:7-8, ELT).

4. You become _____ to them.

5. You have not finished until they pour _____ , what you poured into them.

C. WHAT DOES A DISCIPLE LOOK LIKE?

1. Makes a _____ for salvation. "Then He said to them all, 'If anyone
   desires to come after Me, let him deny himself, and take up his cross daily, and follow Me'" (Luke 9:23).

2. Has a dedication to be _____ . "Christ...leaving us an example
   that we should follow His steps" (1 Peter 2:21).

3. Learns to _____ in Christ. "I am the Vine; you are the branches. He who abides in Me,
   and I in him, bears much fruit; for without Me you can do nothing" (John 15:5).

4. Learns to live by the _____ . "If you abide in My Word, you are My disciples indeed. And you shall know the truth, and the truth will make you free" (John 8:31-32).

5. Knows how to _____ . "If you abide in Me, and My words abide in you, you will ask what you desire, and it shall be done for you" (John 15:7).

6. Makes _____ . "A new commandment I give to you, that you love one another; as I have loved you, that you also love one another" (John 13:34).

7. Testifies to and serves _____ . "Greater love has no one than this, than to lay down one's life for his friends" (John 15:13).

D. HOW DISCIPLE-MAKERS DO IT

1. By _____ . Paul told Timothy, "You have carefully followed My doctrine, manner of life, purpose, faith, longsuffering, love, perseverance, persecution..." (2 Tim. 3:10-11).

"Example is not the main thing; it is the only thing"

—Albert Schweitzer

2. By _____ . Paul called Timothy, "My beloved son" (2 Tim. 1:2).

3. By _____ . Paul sent Timothy to minister in Corinth, Macedonia, Philippi, Thessalonica, etc.

4. By _____ . Timothy heard Paul preach publicly and privately, i.e., "heard of me."

5. By _____ . The two personal letters are reflections of their private conversations.

6. By _____ . Paul listed Timothy's name with his six times. Paul publicly expressed appreciation for Timothy (1 Cor. 4:17), and told the Philippians, "For I have no one like-minded (like Timothy) who will care for your state" (Phil. 2:20).

7. By _____ . Timothy needed a "jump start." "Stir up the gift of God which is in you" (2 Tim. 1:6). "Be strong" (2 Tim. 2:1).

PART FOUR

GRANDPARENTS IN THE BIBLE

POWERPOINT GUIDE

Grandparents In The Bible

By: Elmer Towns

Outlines

Slide 1 of 100

A. LESSONS IN THIS SERIES

- Introduction
- Jacob – a spiritual giver.
- Naomi – a compromising grandmother becomes godly example.
- Asa – a revival grandson came from an ungodly grandmother.
- Noah – a stumbling block.
- Lois – a grandmother overcoming obstacles.
- Paul – a spiritual disciple – making grandfather.

Slide 2 of 100

B. INTRODUCTION

1. The 4/14 window. Most receive Christ between the ages of 4 and 14.

2. There are 50 percent more grandparents today than in 1950.

3. Most become a grandparent at age 47. The youngest grandparent-generation ever.

4. Today's children are a lost generation, who are the rebellious baby boomers, also called a loss generation.

Slide 3 of 100

5. Two myths about grandparenting:
   a. The grandparent's main task is to enjoy grandchildren (not heritage builders).
   b. Grandparenting is a leisure life (not disciplining).

6. According to a survey, very few grandparents feel they are influential.

Slide 4 of 100

---

7. The main task for each generation:

Father/husband	The head (leader) of the family
Mother/wife	The helpmeet
Children	Learn and obey
Grandparent	Heritage

8. 35% American children live in a single parent home. They need grandparents. Some states have 50%.

9. 10% of American children are being raised by grandparents.

Slide 5 of 100

---

10. A larger percentage of grandparents move in with their children to raise grandchildren.

11. Grandparents grieve the loss of their children's marriage.

12. Most grandparents are as clueless about how to influence their grandchildren for God as they were with their own children.

Slide 6 of 100

C. FOUR THINGS GRANDPARENT SHOULD DO

1. Bless their grandchildren. More than money, things or food, give them spiritual security, a significant purpose in life, and sufficient resources.

2. Leave a legacy. When they get the phone call, "Gramps died" what will they remember most about you, and miss the most?

3. Carry the torch, pass it on. The gospel is the torch, don't drop it, hide it, and don't change it.

4. Communicate a standard of moral living in an immoral world. Be their spiritual GPS Gramps.

Slide 7 of 100

D. TEN POINTS OF LIGHT FOR GRANDPARENTS

1. Grandparents can best show a vision of the future. They view the future through the lenses of past failures and successes.

2. Grandparents are effective because they get a second chance.

3. They set a moral example for children and grandchildren. "Life is tough, but it is tougher when you are stupid." ~John Wayne

Slide 8 of 100

---

4. Grandparents are more like God than when they were parents. As parents, produced community, set rules, enforced rules, punished, rewarded. As grandparents: they listen, give good things, fellowship, are patient, show grace, overlook faults, etc. God doesn't mock, put down or criticize.

5. The joy of grandparenting is blessing them, "add value."

6. Grandparents communicate the values and attitudes of tradition by example, gifts, actions, and love. Heritage makers in lives.

Slide 9 of 100

7. How they feel about their grandchildren is how grandchildren will feel about themselves.

8. God has a plan for each grandchild; it is the responsibility of grandparents to help them find it.

9. Grandparents can be the kindest, most patient generation. But a few decide to be crotchety.

10. Grandparents can be a Bridge Over Troubled Water:

Slide 10 of 100

When you're weary, feeling small,
When tears are in your eyes, I will dry them all.
I'm on your side, when times get tough,
And friends just can't be found,
Like a bridge over troubled waters
I will lay me down.

When you're down and out,
When you're on the street,
When evening falls so hard,
I will comfort you,
I will take your hand
When darkness comes,
And pain is all around
Like a bridge over troubled waters
I will lay me down.
~Simon and Garfunkel

Slide 11 of 100

JACOB

THE SPIRITUAL
GIVER

Lesson 2

Slide 12 of 100

A. INTRODUCTION: GENESIS 48:1-22

1. What can a "poor" grandfather give to a son who has everything?

2. What can an absentee grandfather give to children he seldom sees?

3. What can a physically weak grandfather give to his grandchildren?

4. What can a grandfather give, who has nothing left to give?

Slide 13 of 100

B. FOUR THINGS GRANDFATHER SAID TO THEM

1. Jacob told them his testimony. "God Almighty appeared to me at Luz in the land of Canaan" (v. 3). Was this Jacob's salvation experience? "The angel which redeemed me from evil" (v. 16).

WHAT'S INVOLVED IN A TESTIMONY?
What you were like before salvation.
What you did to receive Christ.
How you were changed.

Slide 14 of 100

"God before whom my fathers, Abraham, and Isaac did walk, the God which fed me all my life long until this day" (v. 15).

2. Jacob told them the Word of God. He told them God's name, God's words and God's expectations (vv. 15-17).

3. Jacob told them the four-fold promise of God (v. 4).
   a. Wealth. "Behold I will make thee fruitful."
   b. Influence. "I will multiply thee."
   c. Nation. "I will make of thee a multitude of people."
   d. Land. "I will give this land to thy seed after thee for an everlasting possession."

Slide 15 of 100

OMITTED FROM ABRAHAM'S COVENANT

1. Bless these who bless you.

2. Curse your enemies.

3. Make name great.

Slide 16 of 100

4. Jacob told them about their grandmother. "When I came from Padan, Rachel died by me in the land of Canaan in the way, when yet there was a little way to come to Ephrath, and I buried her there" (v. 7).

    a. Your grandmother died in travel.
    b. I was there when she died.
    c. We were almost home.
    d. She was buried by the road.

C. FOUR THINGS GRANDFATHER DID FOR THEM

1. Jacob adopted them. "Now these two sons, Ephraim and Manasseh . . . are mine" (v. 5). The boys were half Hebrew and half Egyptian.

2. Jacob kissed and hugged them. Jacob showed his affection. "He kissed them and embraced them" (v. 10).

3. Jacob laid his hands on them. "And Israel stretched out his right hand, and laid it upon Ephraim's head, who was the younger, and his left hand upon Manasseh's head, guiding his hands wittingly; for Manasseh was the firstborn" (v. 14). The word *wittingly* means Jacob knew what he was doing.

4. Jacob blessed his grandchildren. "By faith Jacob when he was dying, blessed both the sons of Joseph" (Heb. 11:21).

HOW TO BLESS CHILDREN

Step 1: A meaningful touch.

Step 2: Blessing with a spoken word.

Step 3: Attach high value to the one being blessed.

Step 4: Picture a special future for the one being blessed.

Step 5: An active commitment to fulfilling the blessing.

~From *God Bless You*, by Elmer Towns

D. FOUR THINGS GRANDFATHER GAVE THEM

1. Jacob gave them his name. Jacob adopted the two boys. "They are mine" (v. 5). "Let my name be upon them, and the name of my father Abraham and Isaac" (v. 16).

2. Jacob gave God's future to them. "Let them grow into a multitude in the midst of the earth" (v. 16). "And he blessed them that day, saying, in thee shall Israel bless, saying, God make thee as Ephraim and as Manasseh; and he set Ephraim before Manasseh" (v. 20).

3. Jacob gave them his love.

4. Jacob gave them an example of worship.
    a. The position of worship. "He (Jacob) bowed himself with his face to the earth" (v. 12).
    b. The attitude of worship. "Jacob . . . worshipped, leaning upon the top of his staff" (Heb. 11:21).

E. FOUR LESSONS TO TAKE AWAY

1. Grandparents should be concerned about the spiritual condition of their grandchildren.

2. Grandparents shall be a spiritual example.

3. Grandparents should give their testimony.

4. Grandparents should bless (naturally and spiritually).

NAOMI

A COMPROMISING MOTHER BECOMES A GODLY GRANDMOTHER

Lesson 3

A. HOW NAOMI COMPROMISED

1. She compromised her spiritual priorities.
   a. Did not continue in difficulties. "A famine in the land" (Ruth 1:1).
   b. Enticed by the well-watered plains of Moab (1:1).
   c. Left the Promised Land. "Ephrathites of Bethlehem, Judah" (1:2).

2. She compromised her commitment to the Lord. When Ruth, her daughter-in-law wanted to go with Naomi, she directed her to go back to her foreign god. "Look, your sister-in-law has gone back to her people and to her gods; return after your sister-in-law" (1:15).

3. Naomi compromised her family influence. Naomi's son, Chilion, married outside the faith (1:4).

4. Naomi criticized God's provision for her. "I went out full, and the Lord has brought me home again empty" (1:21).

B. NAOMI'S REPENTANCE SEEN IN HER ACTIONS

1. Naomi recognized God's punishment. Naomi recognized God's punishment. "The Lord hath caused me to suffer, and the Almighty has sent me such tragedy" (1:21, NLB).

2. Naomi's counsel toward family heritage. When Ruth "happened" on Boaz's field, Naomi said, "Blessed be he of the Lord, who has not forsaken His kindness to the living and the dead! And Naomi said to her, this man is a relation of ours, one of our close relatives" (2:20).

3. Naomi counseled toward redemption. "Then Naomi her mother-in- law said unto her, 'My daughter, shall I not seek security for you, that it may be well with you?'" (3:1).

4. Naomi counseled patience and trust. "Then she (Naomi) said, 'Sit still, my daughter . . . for the man will not rest until he has concluded the matter this day'" (3:18).

C. THE BLESSING ON GRANDMOTHER NAOMI

"Then the women said to Naomi, 'Blessed be the Lord, who has not left you this day without a close relative; and may his name be famous in Israel! And may he be to you a restorer of life and a nourisher of your old age; for your daughter-in-law, who loves you, who is better to you than seven sons, has borne him'"
(Ruth 4:14-15).

1. Naomi is given more importance in the Bible than Ruth.
   a. The women blessed Naomi (4:14).
   b. The child is recognized as "kin" to Naomi (4:14).
   c. Naomi had oversight for the child's care (4:16).

2. The child is identified with this grandmother (not father or grandfather). Note: legal line not through Naomi and Elimelech (4:21).

3. The child Obed would be famous in Israel.
   a. The word *famous* means, "name is proclaimed widely."
   b. Obed was the great grandfather of Daniel.
   c. Obed comes from two words, (1) Obadiah i.e., a worshipper of God, (2) *ebed*, i.e., servant. Obed was a true servant and worshipper of the Lord.

4. The child gave Grandmother Naomi a purpose in life.
   a. Naomi had been a compromiser, but she became a woman of conviction.
   b. Naomi didn't have any hope. She told Ruth, "Turn back, my daughters, go-for I am too old to have a husband. If I should say I have hope, if I should have a husband tonight and should also bear sons" (1:12). But God gave her a new life. "He (Obed) shall be unto thee, a restorer of life" (4:15).
   c. Naomi had no spiritual energy. "Call me Mara, for the Almighty hath dealt very bitterly with me" (1:20). But Obed nourished her old age. "And may he (Obed) be to you a restorer of life and a nourisher of your old age" (4:15).

5. Naomi gained the love of her daughter-in-law. "Then the women said to Naomi, 'Blessed be the Lord . . . your daughter-in-law, who loves you, who is better to you than seven sons'" (4:14-15).

6. Naomi had the responsibility of influencing the child.
   a. Naomi was given a second chance to rear a son.
   b. A rich man like Boaz would have a maid for children, i.e., he got Naomi.
   c. "Then Naomi took the child and laid him on her bosom, and became a nurse to him" (4:16).

Slide 33 of 100

ASA

A REVIVAL GRANDSON CAME FROM AN UNGODLY GRANDMOTHER

Lesson 4

Slide 34 of 100

"In the twentieth year of Jeroboam king of Israel, Asa became king over Judah. And he reigned forty-one years in Jerusalem. His grandmother's name was Maachah the granddaughter of Absalom. Asa did what was right in the eyes of the Lord, as did his father David. And he banished the perverted persons from the land, and removed all the idols that his fathers had made. Also, he removed Maachah his grandmother from being queen mother, because she had made an obscene image of Asherah. And Asa cut down her obscene image and burned it by the brook Kidron" (I Kings 15:9-13).

Slide 35 of 100

A. MAACHAH: AN UNGODLY GRANDMOTHER

1. Fighter. Her name Maachah means "fighting" or "oppression."

Slide 36 of 100

2. Rebellious. Maachah was rebellious like her grandfather Absalom. "His (Abijam) mother's name was Maachah, the daughter of Absalom (Absalom)" (1 Kings 15:2).
   a. Absalom murdered his brother Amnon. "Absalom had commanded . . . when I say strike Amnon, then kill him" (2 Sam. 13:28).
   b. Absalom pretended to be loyal to his father David. "So, Absalom stole the hearts of the men of Israel" (2 Sam. 15:6).
   c. Absalom tried to kill his father David. "Make haste to depart from the city of David lest he overtake us suddenly . . . and strike the city with the edge of the sword" (2 Sam. 15:14).

Slide 37 of 100

3. Grandmother Maachah influenced her husband Rehoboam to compromise.
   a. "Rehoboam loved Maachah the daughter of Absalom more than all his wives and his concubines . . . and Rehoboam made Abijah the son of Maachah as chief to be leader over his brethren, for he intended to make him King" (2 Chron. 11:20-22).
   b. Rehoboam's sin split the kingdom.
   c. Rehoboam's continuing sin corrupted the kingdom. "And he (Rehoboam) did evil because he did not prepare his heart to seek the Lord" (2 Chron. 12:14).

Slide 38 of 100

4. Grandmother Maachah gave her son an evil name. The son of Maachah was Abijah (2 Chron. 12:16 ff) whose name means, "The Lord is my Father," but the boy also was given the name Abijam, which means "My father is Yam" a Canaanite god of the sea.

5. Maachah supported sexual sodomy. "And Asa took away all the sodomites out of the land, and removed all the (filthy) idols that his father (Abijam) had made" (1 Kings 15:12).

Slide 39 of 100

6. Maachah worshipped false gods. "Asa removed all the idols that his father and mother had made" (1 Kings 15:12-13, ELT).

7. Maachah secretly had a sexual goddess-idol. She had made an obscene image to Asherah. "And Asa cut down her obscene idol and burned it by the brook Kidron" (1 Kings 15:13).
   a. Idols usually represent a spirit-demon.
   b. Maachah was utterly evil.

Slide 40 of 100

B. ASA, A GODLY GRANDSON

1. Asa reacted to the sins of his father. "Abijam walked in all the sins of his father which he had done before him (evil example), and his heart was not perfect with the Lord his God, or the heart of David" (1 Kings 15:3-4). The principle: extreme abuses lead to reformation.

2. God sovereignly prepared Asa to carry on the godly rule of David. "Nevertheless, for David's sake did the Lord his God give him a lamp in Jerusalem to set up his son (Asa) after him, and to establish Jerusalem" (1 Kings 15:4).

Slide 41 of 100

3. Asa began with reforms (2 Chronicles 14:2-7).
   a. Repented of outward idolatry. "He (Asa) removed the altars of the foreign gods and the high places, and broke down the sacred pillars and cut down the wooden images" (2 Chron. 14:3).
   b. Commanded the people to serve the Lord. "He (Asa) commanded Judah to seek the Lord God of their fathers and to do the law and the commandment" (2 Chron. 14:4).

Slide 42 of 100

c. Asa armed and fortified the nation. "He (Asa) built fortified cities in Judah, for the land had rest; he had no war in those years" (2 Chron. 14:6). "And Asa had an army of three hundred thousand from Judah . . . and from Benjamin two hundred and eighty thousand men" (2 Chron. 14:8).

d. Asa relied on the Lord to defend the nation. When attacked, "Asa cried out to the Lord his God, and said, 'Lord, it is nothing for You to help, whether with many or with those who have no power; help us, O Lord our God, for we rest on You, and in Your name we go against this multitude. O Lord, You are our God; do not let man prevail against You!'" (2 Chron. 14:11).

Slide 43 of 100

4. Asa led the nation in revival (2 Chronicles 15:1-19).
   a. Had the people taught the Scriptures. "For a longtime Israel has been without the true God, without teaching priest, without law" (2 Chron. 15:3).
   b. Reinstituted blood sacrifice. "Restored the altar of the Lord that was before the vestibule of the Lord" (2 Chron. 15:8).
   c. Celebrated the feast to the Lord. "They gathered together at Jerusalem . . . and they offered to the Lord" (2 Chron. 15:10-11).

Slide 44 of 100

d. Led the people in dedication. "They entered into the covenant to seek the Lord God of their fathers with all their heart and with all their soul" (2 Chron. 15:12).

e. Actually, took an oath. "Then they took an oath before the Lord with a loud voice, with shouting, and trumpets, and ram's horn" (2 Chron. 15:14).

Slide 45 of 100

C. LESSONS TO TAKE AWAY

1. Sometimes the sinful excesses in parents and grandparents produce an opposite reaction in children. Notice the conditions when Asa was a child. "There was no peace to the one who went out . . . but great turmoil . . . nation was destroyed by nation, and city by city" (2 Chron. 15:5-6).

2. Sometimes the evil influence of parents produces children more evil than themselves, i.e., Maachah was more evil than Absalom.

Slide 46 of 100

3. Be sure your sin will expose you. Maachah's sin was known and dealt with.

4. Cursed to the third or fourth generation. God had promised, "The Lord thy God is a jealous God, visiting the iniquity of the fathers upon the children to the third and fourth generation of them that hate me" (Ex. 20:5). Absalom →Maachah→Abijam→Asa

Slide 47 of 100

5. God sovereignly raises up righteous children.

6. Sometimes a grandchild has to deal with the sins of a grandparent.

7. A grandchild can become more godly as he/she grows older, i.e., Asa began with reforms, but eventually brought in a revival.

Slide 48 of 100

Noah

WHAT WE KNOW FOR SURE

Lesson 5

Slide 49 of 100

Grandfather – Noah –<u>Sinned</u>

Father – Ham – Gossiped

Grandson – Canaan – <u>Laughed</u>

Slide 50 of 100

"And Noah began to be a farmer, and he planted a vineyard. Then he drank of the wine and was drunk and became uncovered in his tent. And Ham, the father of Canaan, saw the nakedness of his father, and told his two brothers outside. But Shem and Japheth took a garment, laid it on both their shoulders, and went backward and covered the nakedness of their father. Their faces were turned away, and they did not see their father's nakedness. So, Noah awoke from his wine, and knew what his younger son had done to him. Then he said: 'Cursed be Canaan; a servant of servants He shall be to his brethren'" (Gen. 9:20-25).

Slide 51 of 100

1. <u>Godly</u>. What is known about Noah? "Noah was a just man and perfect . . . and Noah walked with God" (Gen. 6:9).

2. <u>Warned of judgment</u>. Why did Noah build an ark? "By faith Noah being divinely warned of things not yet seen moved with godly fear, prepared an ark . . . by which he condemned the world" (Heb. 11:7).

3. <u>Carpenter</u>. What was Noah's occupation? "God said to Noah . . . make yourself an ark of gopher wood" (Gen. 6:14).

Slide 52 of 100

4. <u>Preacher</u>. How did Noah warn the world? "Noah . . . a preacher of righteousness" (2 Peter 2:5).

5. <u>Drinking</u>. What sins did Jesus mention Noah preached against?" As the days of Noah were, so also will be the coming of the Son of Man . . . drinking . . . until the day Noah entered the ark" (Matt. 24:37-38).

Slide 53 of 100

6. <u>Satan worship</u>. What were other sins the people committed? (Gen. 6:1-13).

7. <u>God called</u>. When did Noah enter the ark? "The Lord said to Noah, 'Come thou and all thy house into the ark'" (Gen. 7:1). "He was 601 years old" (Gen. 8:13, NLT).

8. <u>A farmer</u>. What was Noah's new occupation after the flood? "Noah began to be a husbandman and planted a vineyard" (9:20).

Slide 54 of 100

9. What was Noah's threefold sin? "He (Noah) drank of the wine, and was drunken, and he was uncovered within the tent" (Gen. 9:21).
   a. <u>Drunken</u>. He preached against it.
   b. <u>Exposure</u>. He uncovered himself, i.e., *gulah* (reflective).
   c. <u>Lack of role model</u>.

Slide 55 of 100

10. How did Noah know? "Noah awoke from his wine and knew what his younger son had done to him" (9:24).
   a. Special <u>revelation</u>.
   b. <u>Inquiry</u>. He asked or was told.
   c. <u>Memory</u>. A drunk man remembers some things.

Slide 56 of 100

B. WHAT WAS THE SIN OF HAM AND CANAAN?

1. Seeing only. "Ham, the father of Canaan saw the nakedness of his father, and told his two brethren" (Gen. 9:22). What went with seeing?
   a. Lust.
   b. Mockery.
   c. Rejection of father's authority to His God. (Morris)
   d. Not covering, i.e., showing disrespect.

2. Not seeing. "Shem and Japheth took a garment, and laid it upon their shoulders, and went backward, and covered the nakedness of their father . . . . and saw not their father's nakedness" (Gen. 9:23).

3. Why curse Canaan?
   a. Youngest. Ham was the youngest son of Noah, and Canaan youngest son of Ham (Gen. 10:6).
   b. Divine curse. This was not an "angry" grandfather. Since only God could know the future, Noah spoke by God's revelation. God cursed Canaan for what he did, and what He was to become.
   c. Noah recognized a rebellious attitude and perverse lust. Noah/God saw a weakness in Canaan and knew it would be perpetuated.
   d. Third generation always suffers the most, "cursed be Canaan, a servant of servants, shall he be to his brethren" (Gen. 9:25).

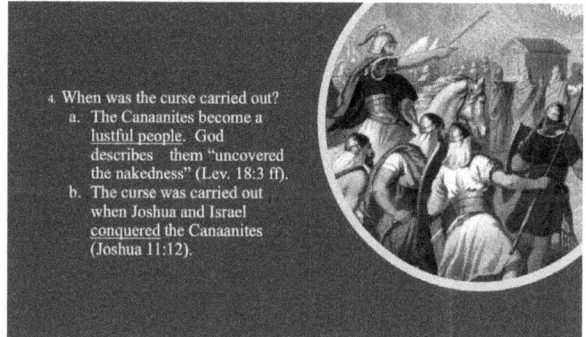

4. When was the curse carried out?
   a. The Canaanites become a lustful people. God describes them "uncovered the nakedness" (Lev. 18:3 ff).
   b. The curse was carried out when Joshua and Israel conquered the Canaanites (Joshua 11:12).

C. WHAT LESSONS CAN BE LEARNED ABOUT SINNING GRANDPARENTS

1. You never get too old to quit sinning.

2. You can fall at your greatest strength. "Let him that thinketh he standeth take heed lest he fall" (1 Cor. 10:12).

3. Your fall can hurt your family. "Cursed be Canaan."

4. Your fall can come after God has greatly used you. Noah, Elijah, Peter, Paul, Uriah, David.

5. Just because you have done a lot for God, doesn't mean He will overlook your sin in old age.

6. The careless root of sin in a grandfather or father (lust or rebellion) can have disastrous results in grandchildren.

7. Drunkenness is not a private sin, nor is it something God overlooks.

8. The body is the temple of the Holy Spirit, and the child of God should be modest.
   a. Applies to all ages.
   b. Applies to sexual exposure.
   c. Applies to sexual viewing, i.e., lust.

9. Hitherto repressed lust and sexual fantasies will surface when given the opportunity.

D. WHAT GRANDPARENTS AND GRANDCHILDREN NEED TO KNOW

1. God provides victory. "No temptation has overtaken you except such as is common to man; but God is faithful, who will not allow you to be tempted beyond what you are able, but with the temptation will also make the way of escape, that you may be able to bear it" (1 Cor. 10:13).

2. God lives in your body. "He who commits sexual immorality, sins against his own body. Do you not know that your body is the temple of the Holy Spirit, who is in you . . . you are not your own" (1 Cor. 6:18-19).

3. Old age sin will disqualify you. "But I discipline my body and bring it into subjection, lest, when I have preached to others, I myself should become disqualified" (1 Cor. 9:27).

Slide 65 of 100

LOIS

A GRANDMOTHER OVERCOMING OBSTACLES

Lesson 6

Slide 66 of 100

A. LOIS: LIVING BEYOND HER CIRCUMSTANCES

1. Married a Gentile just as her daughter Eunice. "Timothy, the son of a certain Jewish woman (Eunice) who believed, but his father was a Greek" (Acts 16:1).

2. What was her life in Lystra?
   a. Not enough Jewish families for a Synagogue.
   b. Not any civilized advantage.
   c. Not many Roman citizens.

Slide 67 of 100

3. Lois expected a son but got a daughter. "Thy grandmother Lois, and thy mother Eunice" (2 Tim. 1:3).

4. Lois became a genuine believer. Paul said, "I call to remembrance the unfeigned faith that is in you (Timothy), which dwelt first in your grandmother Lois" (2 Tim. 1:5). Unfeigned means genuine, not a play actor repeating lines.

Slide 68 of 100

5. Lois and Eunice poured their faith into Timothy. "Continue in the things which you (Timothy) have been assured, knowing for whom you have learned them" (2 Tim. 3:14).
   a. The word "whom" is plural, both taught.
   b. The word "knowing" is *oida*, i.e., innate knowledge. Their teaching becomes more than knowledge, it became his conviction.
   c. The word "continue" means the women laid a foundation on which Paul and Timothy built.

Slide 69 of 100

6. Lois and Eunice began teaching early. "That from childhood you have known the Holy Scriptures, which are able to make you wise for salvation" (2 Tim. 3:15).
   a. The word "childhood" is *brephos*, which means embryo or newborn baby.
   b. The word "known" is *oida*, i.e., innate knowledge.
   c. Holy Scriptures is *braphe*, i.e., writings, which is plural all parts of the Word of God.
   d. "Make you wise into" Greek suggests "motion into." The women were moving Timothy into salvation.

Slide 70 of 100

7. The women prepared the spiritual foundation for Timothy's conversion. "When I (Paul), call to remembrance the unfeigned faith that is in you, which dwelt first in your grandmother Lois and your mother Eunice, and I am persuaded is in you also" (2 Tim. 1:5).

Slide 71 of 100

B. PAUL BUILT ON LOIS AND EUNICE

1. The women were converted on Paul's first trip. (Acts 14:6-23). Paul returned on his second trip. "Then he came to Derbe and Lystra, and behold a certain disciple was there, named Timothy, the son of a certain Jewish woman who believed, but his father was a Greek" (Acts 16:1). "Believed" is past tense.

2. Timothy believed in Christ under Paul's ministry. "To Timothy, my true son in the faith" (1 Tim. 1:2). "To Timothy my beloved son" (2 Tim. 1:2).

Slide 72 of 100

3. Timothy believed in spite of persecution. "The Jews . . . stoned Paul and dragged him out of the city (Lystra) supposing him to be dead" (Acts 14:19). Timothy was probably an eyewitness. "You have fully known my doctrine, manner of life . . . persecutions, afflictions, which came upon me at Antioch, at Iconium, at Lystra" (2 Tim. 3:10-11).

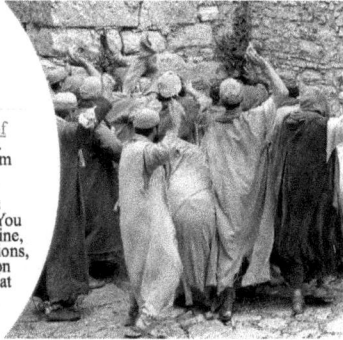

Slide 73 of 100

4. Timothy was recommended by the church leaders at Lystra. "Do not neglect the gift that is in you . . . with the laying on of hands of the presbytery" (1 Tim. 4:14). They would have endorsed the training given by Lois and Eunice.

5. Timothy was ordained by Paul. "Stir up the gift of God which is in you through the laying on of my hands" (2 Tim. 1:6).

Slide 74 of 100

C. LESSONS TO TAKE AWAY

1. When a grandmother has many limitations, she can be a great influence for God through your children.

2. Godly children are not automatically raised.
It takes:
a. Early instruction
b. Plain instruction
c. Frequent instruction
d. Patient instruction

• (Adapted from John Wesley)

Slide 75 of 100

3. Your home can be a great godly influence, even when a church is not available to help.

4. Every grandmother should get the help of a godly role model to influence her grandchildren.

5. Giving attention to small details in a child's education will influence his/her total life.

6. When grandparents can't be all they want to be in life, at least they can be faithful in what's given them in life.

Slide 76 of 100

Unknown Grandsons

Lesson 5

Slide 77 of 100

A. THREE GENERATIONS DOWN

1. From rags to riches to rags in three generations.

Grandfather: poor but worked hard for money.

Son: enjoyed riches but didn't earn them.

Grandson: lazy and lost all.

Slide 78 of 100

2. From sin to salvation to sin in three generations.
Grandfather: wicked but gloriously transformed from sin.
Son: enjoyed Christianity but lived on father's faith.
Grandson: enticed by sin, then corrupted by sin.

3. From slavery to the Lord to slavery in three generations.
Grandfather Caleb: Slave but great character.
Son-in-law Othniel: Attacked but survived.
Unknown grandson: Loved sin, then a slave.

Slide 79 of 100

4. The compromising unknown grandsons: what they forgot, what they changed, what they lost.

"And the people served the Lord all the days of Joshua (and Caleb), and all they days of the elders (and Othniel) that outlived Joshua . . . there was another generation after them that knew not the Lord . . . they did evil in the sight of the Lord, and served Baalim . . . and the anger of the Lord was against them and he delivered them into the hands of the nations round about them"
(Judges 2:7-13, ELT).

Slide 80 of 100

B. WHAT THEY FORGOT

1. They forgot they had been slaves that God delivered.

2. They forgot God guided them through the Red Sea and the desert.

3. They forgot God gave them the Promised Land.

Slide 81 of 100

C. WHAT THEY CHANGED

1. They changed their God for idols.

2. They changed their opinion about themselves. They no longer saw themselves as delivered slaves, but as satisfied plantation owners.

3. They changed their relationship to sin. They no longer separated from the enemy, but took them as house-servants, then intermarried with them.

Slide 82 of 100

D. WHAT THEY LOST

1. They lost their pioneering spirit. "They did not drive them out (Judges 1:32).

2. They lost their conviction of belief. "They forsook the Lord and served Baal" (Judges 2:13).

3. They lost their desire for separation from sin. "They turned quickly from the way in which their fathers walked" (Judges 2:17).

Slide 83 of 100

E. FIRST GENERATION: CALEB

1. Knew God had freed him from slavery in Egypt.

2. Knew God led him from Egypt through the Red Sea.

3. Knew God gave him his possessions. "Therefore, give me this mountain, whereof the Lord spoke in that day" (Joshua 14:12). "But my servant Caleb . . . hath followed me fully, him will I bring into the land to possess it" (Num. 14:24).

Slide 84 of 100

F. SECOND GENERATION: OTHNIEL

"And he (Caleb) gave him (Othniel) Achsah his daughter to wife" (Joshua 15:17).

"The children of Israel served Chushanrishathaim eight years. When the children of Israel cried . . . the Lord raised up a deliver . . . Othniel" (Judges 3:8-9).

Slide 85 of 100

1. Othniel's generation lost their pioneering spirit. "The children of Israel dwelt among the Canaanites" (Judges 3:5).

2. Othniel's generation lost their beliefs. "Forgot the Lord their God" (Judges 3:7).

3. Othniel's generation lost their separation from sin. "Took their daughters to be their wives" (Judges 3:6).

Slide 86 of 100

G. WHAT THE THIRD GENERATION: GRANDSONS MUST DO

1. Must be wise to recognize sin. "The Lord left to prove Israel . . . even as many as had not known the wars of Canaan" (Judges 3:3-5, ELT).

2. Must be strong to fight sin. "These nations . . . the Lord allows to stay . . . to teach Israel to fight" (Judges 3:1, ELT).

Slide 87 of 100

3. Must have conviction to follow the Lord. "They were to prove Israel . . . to know whether they (Israel) would harken unto the commandments of the Lord" (Judges 3:4).

Slide 88 of 100

Paul

**A SPIRITUAL
GRANDFATHER
A DISCIPLE-MAKING
GRANDPARENT**

Lesson 7

Slide 89 of 100

"And the things that you have heard from me among many witnesses, commit these to faithful men who will be able to teach others also"
(2 Tim. 2:2).

Spiritual Grandfather – Paul – Disciple-maker
Son in ministry – Timothy – Learner
Third Generation – Faithful men – Passed lessons on
Fourth Generation – Others – The proof of Christianity

Slide 90 of 100

A. WHAT GRANDPARENTS DO THAT PARENTS DON'T DO

1. Grandparents make you feel grown up, while parents treat you as a child.

2. Grandparents can deal with positive gentleness, while parents must deal with negative consequences.

3. Grandparents point out your future greatness, while parents must deal with your present shortcomings.

Slide 91 of 100

4. Grandparents can build individual initiative, while parents must deal with your personal responsibility and accountability.

5. Grandparents have learned what is eternally important and can overlook immediate issues.

Slide 92 of 100

B. WHAT IS A DISCIPLE-MAKING GRANDPARENT?

1. You are a reproducer of reproducers.
   a. Because children are mimickers, they live out your examples.
   b. How you influence them is how they will be grandparents for future generations.

Paul
   Timothy
      Faithful men
         Others

Slide 93 of 100

2. Your life will outlive your lessons.

3. You pour your soul into them. "As apostles of Christ . . . we were gentle among you as a parent cherishing a baby . . . giving you not only the gospel, but we poured our own lives into you" (1 Thess. 2:7-8, ELT).

4. You become necessary to them.

5. You have not finished until they pour into others, what you poured into them.

Slide 94 of 100

C. WHAT DOES A DISCIPLE LOOK LIKE?

1. Makes a radical decision for salvation. "Then He said to them all, 'If anyone desires to come after Me, let him deny himself, and take up his cross daily, and follow Me'" (Luke 9:23).

2. Has a dedication to be like Jesus. "Christ . . . leaving us an example that we should follow His steps" (1 Peter 2:21).

Slide 95 of 100

3. Learns to abide in Christ. "I am the Vine; you are the branches. He who abides in Me, and I in him, bears much fruit; for without Me you can do nothing" (John 15:5).

4. Learns to live by the Scriptures. "If you abide in My Word, you are My disciples indeed. And you shall know the truth, and the truth will make you free" (John 8:31-32).

5. Knows how to pray. "If you abide in Me, and My words abide in you, you will ask what you desire, and it shall be done for you" (John 15:7).

Slide 96 of 100

6. By promotion. Paul listed Timothy's name with his six times. Paul publicly expressed appreciation for Timothy (1 Cor. 4:17), and told the Philippians, "For I have no one like-minded (like Timothy) who will care for your state" (Phil. 2:20).

7. By prodding. Timothy needed a "jump start." "Stir up the gift of God which is in you" (2 Tim. 1:6). "Be strong" (2 Tim. 2:1).

6. Makes love the distinguishing mark of life. "A new commandment I give to you, that you love one another; as I have loved you, that you also love one another" (John 13:34).

7. Testifies to and serves others. "Greater love has no one than this, than to lay down one's life for his friends" (John 15:13).

D. HOW DISCIPLE-MAKERS DO IT

1. By example. Paul told Timothy, "You have carefully followed My doctrine, manner of life, purpose, faith, longsuffering, love, perseverance, persecution . . ." (2 Tim. 3:10-11).

"Example is not the main thing; it is the only thing"
~Albert Schweitzer

2. By association. Paul called Timothy, "My beloved son" (2 Tim. 1:2).

3. By assignment. Paul sent Timothy to minister in Corinth, Macedonia, Philippi, Thessalonica, etc.

4. By instruction. Timothy heard Paul preach publicly and privately, i.e., "heard of me."

5. By private counsel. The two personal letters are reflections of their private conversations.

PART FIVE

GRANDPARENTS IN THE BIBLE

ADDITIONAL RESOURCES

POWERPOINT SLIDES:

To purchase and download the Powerpoint Slides go to
https://www.norimediagroup.com/pages/elmer-towns

VIDEO:

To purchase available video by Dr Towns go to
https://www.norimediagroup.com/pages/elmer-towns

ADD-ON CONTENT

To purchase additional products in this series go to
https://www.norimediagroup.com/pages/elmer-towns

RELATED BOOKS

Available at https://www.norimediagroup.com/pages/elmer-towns

www.ingramcontent.com/pod-product-compliance
Lightning Source LLC
Chambersburg PA
CBHW062038090426
42740CB00016B/2948